WHERE to RETIRE in MAINE

Victoria Doudera

DOWN EAST BOOKS
ROCKPORT, MAINE

ISBN 0-89272-597-4
LCCN: 2002109175
Printed at Versa Press, E. Peoria, Ill.

5   4   3   2   1

Down East Books
A division of Down East Enterprise, Inc.,
Publisher of *Down East*, the Magazine of Maine

Book orders: 1-800-685-7962
www.downeastbooks.com

Contents

Introduction

When Claudia Fortin told her friends in Pennsylvania that she was retiring to central Maine, one woman was so surprised she nearly choked on the currant scone she was chewing. "These women all acted as if I were moving to Antarctica," says Claudia. "They wondered what I would do up here, and how in the world I would ever survive the winters." But Claudia and her husband, Joe, had vacationed for years on pristine Sebec Lake, where they knew several townspeople and belonged to a small church.

"We have always loved Maine," she recounts, "and we knew it was where we wanted to spend our retirement years. We weren't interested in a Disneyland kind of existence. We wanted something real, and safe, and friendly. We wanted to take walks with the dog at night and not be afraid. And visit the hardware store and be on a first-name basis with the owner. So we moved north, and now those same Pittsburgh friends visit and do not want to leave."

To some people living beyond Maine's borders, the idea of retirement in our northeasternmost state almost seems laughable. After all, the typical retiree wants nonstop sunshine, a gated community, and an all-you-can-eat early-bird buffet, right? Wrong! Just as the image of the rocking-chair-bound senior citizen is as outdated as a Cadillac without power windows, the concept of the "ideal" retirement haven no longer suits some retirees. What *do* people really want when they contemplate retirement? Can Maine, with its pine-scented forests, white-steepled churches, and, yes, snowy winters, really be in the running?

Choosing a new community requires weighing many factors, all of them significant. Considerations such as the location of family and friends, the availability of specialized health care, and the cost of living all play key roles. Low crime rates, respected medical facilities, convenient airports—these are qualities many of us desire. What about friendly neighbors, well-stocked libraries, and uncrowded roads? Assets such as these are tremendously important and contribute to a community's vibrancy and charm. Small-town living is another desirable characteristic: while it's nice to live near a big city, most of us yearn for the kind of place where Jimmy Stewart would feel right at home.

As increasing numbers of people are discovering, retirement in the great state of Maine can mean all of these things and much more. Pleasant neighbors, safe streets, outdoor activities, and varied cultural offerings are just part of what makes the state special. Top-notch health care, new retirement villages, and a clean, simple lifestyle are also part of the allure. As long as your dreams don't include tropical jungles, chances are good you can find your ideal place to retire in the Pine Tree State, and this book can help guide you to that spot.

Consider a few statistics. Maine's tax records reveal that the number of retirees moving into the state is double the number of retirement-age folks moving out. Just as telling, ninety-five percent of Maine's residents who are fifty-five and older plan to spend their retirement here, in their home state, not in warmer climes to the south. Maine is not only "in the running" when it comes to retirement locations, but is—for a variety of reasons—quietly becoming the premier such destination in the Northeast.

My first book, *Moving to Maine: The Essential Guide to Get You There* (Down East Books, 2000), describes what life is like in the state of Maine and offers an insider's look at how the state works, plays, and survives mud season. If you are not yet familiar with Maine, or if you want to learn everything from how to register your boat to where to spot a moose, I recommend finding a copy.

Where to Retire in Maine has a different focus. It gives an in-depth look at nearly two dozen Maine communities, providing essential information especially tailored to those considering retirement. Facts about health care availability, transportation, safety, traffic, and housing options are included, as well as details concerning fitness, educational, cultural, and shopping opportunities. Practical information such as local newspapers, Web sites, and volunteer organizations are also listed for each community, as are long-term care facilities, retirement villages, area churches, libraries, and airports. Along with facts and figures, I've tried to capture the flavor of each community, through my own observations as well as the comments of people who actually live there.

Although *Where to Retire in Maine* profiles many of the state's most desirable locations, it is my belief that numerous Maine locales fit the retirement bill nicely. From way up in Fort Kent to down south

One of Maine's larger residents. PHOTO COURTESY OF THE RANGELEY LAKES CHAMBER OF COMMERCE

in quaint York, towns here are safe, friendly, and surprisingly active when it comes to culture and recreation. Even Maine's cities have a small-town feel, and even its smallest villages have libraries linked to the Internet.

And now for the ultimate question: what about the weather?

It's true that Maine's fabled four-season climate can deliver some whopping storms. It's also a fact that the weather differs in various parts of the state, as I explain in greater detail in the *About This Book* section. Nevertheless, Maine is surely no notch in the Sunbelt, and no matter how much the globe warms, we probably won't be wearing shorts at Christmastime. If your idea of dressing for winter means flinging a golf sweater over your shoulders, you'd better set your sights on warmer climes.

But if you enjoy seeing the sugar maples crimson against the sky, or spotting wild turkeys in a farmer's field, or getting to know your neighbors, or leaving your car doors unlocked, then maybe Maine's for you. If you can live for much of the year without glitzy malls and congested highways but want an active, engaging retirement, perhaps this is your place. Whether you want to learn new skills, hone old interests, explore wild places, or simply relax, you can do it in Maine, and I hope this book guides you on your journey.

Please don't hesitate to contact me with your feedback and questions. Since *Moving to Maine: The Essential Guide to Get You There* was published, I've indulged my love of Maine houses and become a realtor. If I can assist you in your search for the perfect home, give me a call at 207-236-6171, or e-mail me at <u>Vicki@camdenre.com</u>. I look forward to hearing from you.

▲▲▲

About This Book

I could retire just about anywhere in Maine. I can imagine myself in Eastport, rising with the sun and taking brisk hikes along the craggy cliffs. I could make a home in Waterville, where I'd shop for bargains at Marden's department store and audit courses at Colby College. And wouldn't life be pleasant up in Houlton? I'd stroll by beautiful old homes built by lumber barons on my way to watch movies in the newly refurbished Temple Theatre.

Maine has so many special places that it was difficult to choose only twenty-one communities. I agonized for months before coming up with a system to help with the selection, and even then I waffled. I know there are some wonderful towns that I have not profiled, and I deeply regret their omission. I hope you'll let me know through Down East Books about specific Maine locales that you feel would be worthwhile additions to future editions.

⬆ THE COMMUNITIES

This book portrays towns and cities in Maine that possess qualities shown to matter most to retirees. Assets such as competent and convenient health care, educational opportunities, cultural diversions, recreational facilities, and outgoing residents were some of the criteria used to choose the communities. Included as well are places with Main Streets that are healthy, thriving, and attractive. Many of the towns offer choices for retirement living: independent living communities, active-adult condominium developments, and congregate-care facilities. That said, there are profiles as well of villages that are on the quieter side, that offer more in the way of peace and quiet than programs and conveniences. One is an island the size of Manhattan with very little commercial activity but a whole lot of civic pride. The other is a four-season destination with outstanding scenery, outdoor activities, and more moose than men.

Accompanying each community are statistics taken from the Maine Census Data Program and Maine Census Consortium, a part of the United States Census 2000 project. Used in both the "At a Glance" and "Who Lives Here" sections, these figures give a snapshot of the demographics of each place. I've included the obvious numbers such as population and land area, as well as median age, percentage over age sixty-two, median household income, and the like. If you need more detailed information on a particular community, it's available online at http://censtats.census.gov/pub/Profiles.shtml. (Select "Maine," enter an asterisk in the next box, then click "Go.")

▲ WEATHER

Maine weather is best described by one word: changeable. A sunny morning can be followed by a rainy afternoon; a summer day of almost tropical heat can follow a cool, foggy one. As one retiree remarked to me, the weather here varies not only from day to day, but from year to year.

Meteorologists say the Maine climate is affected by several factors. Nearness to the ocean, which tends to temper weather, is a major influence on any coastal community's climate. North American storm tracks, which converge on New England and Maritime Canada, also loom large in determining what kind of precipitation we can expect. Finally, air masses from source regions such as tropical oceans, continental interiors, the sub-Arctic, and the cool ocean surface to the east shape the day's forecast. These factors influence us singly but also interact to make for a dynamic weather pattern that is frequently very different from one corner of Maine to the other.

The most famous of storms here is called a "nor'easter."

According to weather experts, this system moves off the continent south of Maine, then advances slowly across the Gulf of Maine with winds spinning counterclockwise. These moisture-laden winds blow over the coastal portion of the state from a northeasterly direction, bringing buckets of summer rain and blankets of winter snow.

In the Weather section for each community, I give the average temperatures for January, April, July, and October as well as the average annual rainfall and snowfall as listed by the National Oceanic and Atmospheric Administration/National Climatic Data Center for the past decade. Even with this information, it is impossible to capture on paper the beauty and variety of our changeable Maine climate. Suffice it to say that residents are adept at handling whatever Mother Nature dishes out.

↟ TAXES

It stands to reason that the cost of living matters greatly to retirees, and, within that framework, taxes are a huge concern. Below are state and federal taxes applicable in Maine. Without a doubt it is the property tax—the oldest form of taxation in Maine—that vexes new Mainers, and some long-term residents, the most.

General Sales Tax: 5%

Gas Tax: 19 cents per gallon

Telecommunications Property Tax: 27 mills

Rooms and Meals: 7%

Alcohol in Restaurants: 7%

Alcohol in Stores: 6%

Auto Rentals: 10%

Low-Energy Fuels: 8 cents per gallon

Diesel Fuel: 20 cents per gallon

Personal Income: 2 to 8.5%

Cigarettes: 74 cents on a pack of 20

State income tax: For married couples filing jointly, the rate is graduated from 2% of taxable income up to $8,250, to 8.5% on amounts over $33,000. For single filers, it is graduated from 2% of taxable income up to $4,150, to 8.5% on amounts over $16,500.

Income tax exemptions: Social Security benefits are exempt. There is an exemption for pension income of up to $6,000 per person of the amount included in federal adjusted gross income. This exemption must be reduced by the amount of any Social Security benefits received.

Estate tax: None, except the state's "pick-up" portion of the federal tax, applicable to taxable estates of more than $1 million (as of 2002).

Property tax rate: Each Maine municipality has its own property tax, levied according to a mill rate, which is the dollars/cents per $1,000 of value due in property taxes. Both *real* (land and buildings) and *personal* property (tangible goods) are subject to taxation, unless they are exempted by law or subject to another form of taxation, such as the excise tax for motor vehicles and boats. Just what do Maine's much-maligned property taxes fund? Nearly three-fourths of the cost of local government services, which, even in Maine's smallest communities, adds up to a heck of a lot of things. Municipalities in Maine fund their local schools and provide police and fire protection, winter and summer road maintenance, code enforcement, planning, economic and community development, issuance of licenses, recreation, parking, solid waste collection and disposal, water and sewer services, emergency medical services, health and human services, and sometimes even more.

Maine's homestead exemption subtracts $7,000 from the assessed value of a home. There are also property tax and rent refunds for low-income and elderly residents.

Assessing property in Maine: Local assessors use three methods to determine a property's worth. One technique bases worth on the selling prices of similar types of property. A second method determines how much it would take at the current price of materials and labor to replace a building, then subtracts how much the building has depreciated. The third strategy evaluates how much income the property would produce if it were rented, like an apartment house, store, or factory. One, two, or all three of these methods might be used to help the assessor determine the fair market value of a property. Keep in mind that land and buildings are valued separately. Therefore, a home with water frontage may be assessed at a significantly higher value, because of the land's value, than an identical home without water frontage.

Along with each community's property tax rate, I've included a percentage called the ratio to current market value. According to John McGinley, assessor for the town of Rangeley, this percentage represents the assessed value of a property versus its sale value. In any town, this number depends on the location of the property as well as the cycle of revaluation updates in the town.

⬆ REAL ESTATE

From old sea captains' mansions to new shingle-style condos, Maine is a state of many types of dwellings. Few places have as many historic homes, and few states have as many (nearly 1,200) listed in the National Register of Historic Places.

For each community profiled in *Where to Retire in Maine*, I asked a local real estate broker to estimate the cost of older homes, new homes, water- or riverfront homes, lots, and apartments. In some cases, I've indicated where certain types of houses are just not an option. Although rents are included, Maine is notoriously low in rental apartments and homes, a problem many communities are working hard to address.

I am grateful to these professionals for their time and thoughtful comments. Please keep in mind that their estimates are subject to change and are included for comparison's sake only.

♠ RETIREMENT LIVING

Maine has a number of high-quality retirement communities of all stripes, located along the coast and in some inland locations. Some offer a range of housing options and on-site service, while others are active-adult communities geared to empty-nesters ready to leave snow shoveling behind. For each locale, I have included retirement communities in and around town. A complete list of all Maine's retirement communities is found in the Appendix.

♠ PUBLIC SAFETY

A low crime rate is one of the top selling points for any community, and Maine, with its extremely low levels of illegal activity, repeatedly places among the country's safest states. For each town or city in this book, I interviewed the police chief or other high-ranking official to gain a sense of the community's level of safety. Included as well are Uniform Crime Reporting statistics citing the number of crimes per 1,000 population in each town from January through December 2000. The Uniform Crime Reporting (UCR) program is a nationwide cooperative effort by more than 16,000 city, county, and state law enforcement agencies that voluntarily provide data on reported crimes. Criminal activity in some Maine towns is practically nil! In such cases, I've included UCR data for the county in which the towns are located. Please keep in mind that these numbers are larger than what the towns themselves would report. For more information, see www.state.me.us/dps/cim/crime_in_maine/2000pdf/!90count.pdf.

♠ HEALTH CARE

Maine has forty-one acute care and specialty hospitals as well as several government-run and military-related facilities. Despite Maine's rural nature, you can be fairly well assured that quality health care and state-of-the-art facilities are never far away. Even with a relatively high rate of cigarette smoking (an issue the state is diligently addressing), Maine consistently ranks as one of the healthiest states in the country. Perhaps this is due to the kind of personalized care residents receive in hospitals and medical practices, as well as the exceptional professionals Maine's medical community recruits. Or maybe we're just vigorous souls.

For each community profiled, I've described the town's hospital or closest medical facility as well as any other types of health care options, such as assisted living, long-term care, hospice, and emergency clinics. Many of these facilities have informative Web sites offering further details.

♣ CONTINUING EDUCATION

Want to build a wooden boat? Converse in French? Design a Web site? Educational opportunities of every type are available throughout Maine. One of the most exciting ideas to come down the pike is the concept of Senior College, fourteen learning centers scattered around the state that offer older Mainers a variety of courses on topics from the practical to the whimsical, from abstract to hands-on. Nationwide there are hundreds of institutes for senior learning, but Maine has the distinction of being the first to support a statewide institute of learning for learning's sake.

In 2002, some 3,600 students at Maine's new network of senior colleges took classes ranging from Abraham Lincoln to abstract geometry. Limited to people 55 and older, the six- to eight-week-long courses are taught mainly by seniors themselves and bear out the notion that retirees needn't retire their minds. "Senior college is an exciting, compelling idea for people for whom education has been a value their whole lives," says Kali Lightfoot, director of the Portland-based college at the University of Southern Maine, the Osher Lifelong Learning Institute. Lightfoot also oversees the statewide network and says "it's thriving."

Included in this section is the location of the closest senior college for each community profiled. For more information, call 800-800-4USM, ext. 8181, or visit www.usm.maine.edu/eap/seniorcollege.

Also included under Continuing Education are nearby colleges and universities as well as adult education programs offered either through the town or the local school system. Newcomers to Maine are constantly surprised at the amount and variety of courses offered at their local high school. Residents of some Maine communities also have the option of auditing courses at selected colleges, so be sure to investigate whether this is an option in the town you choose.

In addition to the educational offerings described in this section, here are two more options. Elderhostel, an international program, delivers courses year-round in Maine. Call 1-877-426-8056, or visit www.elderhostel.org. CyberSeniors, a computer learning center, offers classes at many learning centers throughout Maine. Call 1-888-676-6622, or www.cyberseniors.org.

♠ LIBRARIES AND HISTORICAL SOCIETIES

Because a good library is so important, I've included for each community both a listing and a longer sidebar detailing the history of, and current offerings at, each town's public library. "Libraries become a central meeting place in a community," notes Bill Byrnes of Newcastle Square Realty in midcoast Maine. "Libraries host classes, provide computer access, and offer services such as book groups and reading programs. They're tremendously important in any Maine town."

Historical societies are another important resource, both as a fount of information about an area and as a way to connect with others who share an interest in the past. Maine loves its history, and even the smallest towns are apt to have a historical exhibit or two.

Whenever possible, I've included contact information for these important organizations.

⬥ SPECIFICALLY FOR SENIORS

This heading refers to any programs that a community might offer—clubs, gatherings, outings—for the sole purpose of bringing senior Mainers together. Many towns have very active programs, housed in their own buildings, while others rely on churches or other organizations to provide these services.

⬥ VOLUNTEERING

Maine offers almost unlimited volunteer opportunities and genuinely welcomes those wishing to get involved. Whatever your interest, be it conservation or commerce, there is an organization that could use your time and expertise. I've given a small sampling from the many choices available in each town; keep in mind that town boards and committees also encourage participation, although it's a good idea to get the lay of the land before putting forth too many suggestions.

⬥ RECREATION

Tennis, anyone? Opportunities to enjoy sports such as tennis, golf, and skiing, as well as outdoor pursuits such as hunting, fishing, and hiking, are what Maine is all about. A recent survey found that sixty-five percent of Maine's older residents want an active, energetic retirement. Fortunately, the options for outdoor recreation are almost limitless in Maine, and I've done my best to give a sense of the possibilities in each community. (Truthfully, this information could fill a book on its own!) Also included here are local town and state parks, where many other activities (swimming, birding, and daydreaming) can take place.

♠ ENTERTAINMENT

Although Maine is considered a rural state, the towns and cities within this book contain a surprising number of diversions such as cinemas, museums, and theaters. "I am always amazed at the variety of concerts, plays, and films available in this part of down east Maine," says a retiree in Ellsworth. Whenever possible, I've included contact information and a Web address so you can gather even more cultural facts.

♠ NATURE

Conservation areas, preserves, and botanical gardens are listed in this section. Not mentioned is the fact that much of Maine—even the more populated southern counties—has acres and acres of wild, natural landscape for those who appreciate flora and fauna.

♠ SHOPPING

Grocery stores are vital in any community, but just as important are the handy shops that carry essentials such as hardware, medicine, and a good bottle of Merlot. While Maine is blessedly free of the miles of strip malls that plague so much of America, nevertheless you can shop here, and we do have some top-quality stores, both large and small. Malls may be a distance from many communities, but smaller stores where you're apt to be greeted by the owner him- or herself contribute to a small-town, neighborly feeling.

♠ WHO LIVES HERE

As mentioned earlier, these statistics are taken from the Maine Census Data Program and Maine Census Consortium, a part of the United States Census 2000 project.

♠ ESSENTIAL PHONE NUMBERS AND WEB SITES

Contact information for the town office or city hall, chamber of commerce, and other related organizations are listed here.

▲ LOCAL NEWS

One of the best ways to learn about a community is through its local paper. In addition to these dailies and weeklies, many towns now have Web sites, produced either by the town or by an eager resident, and I've included these as well.

▲ TRANSPORTATION

While the car is the main mode of transportation in the Pine Tree State, many communities are not far from bus and even train service. There are thirty-six airports and landing strips in Maine; I've included the closest one for each community profiled.

▲ DISTANCE TO OTHER CITIES

Kathie Slowikowski at AAA in Portland provided the mileage from each community to the cities of Portland, Bangor, Boston, New York, Montreal, and Quebec City.

▲ JOBS

This section gives a snapshot of each community's economic picture, using the Labor Market Area's annual figures for 2001. According to the Bureau of Labor Statistics, U.S. Department of Labor, a labor market area consists of "an economically integrated geographical area within which workers can reside and find employment within a reasonable distance or can readily change employment without changing their place of residence." I've included the size of the work-force, the numbers employed and unemployed, and the unemployment rate.

▲ UTILITIES

Are Internet service providers considered utilities? I've grouped them with electricity, water, telephone, and all of the other essentials of day-to-day life.

▲ PLACES OF WORSHIP

In writing this book, I was struck by how many newcomers mentioned churches as one of the key ways to get connected in a Maine community. While I have not listed all of the houses of worship in the towns profiled, I've tried to give a sense of the number and variety of spiritual centers.

▲ EVENTS AND FESTIVALS

A good fair or festival is the highlight of a Maine summer, and fortunately, many towns around the state sponsor not one event, but several! In addition to the nostalgia of an old-fashioned country fair, many towns offer musical, theatrical, and even political events.

▲ RESTAURANTS AND LODGING

These sections give a sampling of what's available in terms of hotels, motels, bed-and-breakfasts, and restaurants in each community profiled. I wish I could say that I've stayed and eaten at each of these businesses, but I haven't. Because I have no firsthand experience with them, I offer only examples, not recommendations.

▲ WHAT THE LOCALS SAY

This section of each town profile shares information gleaned from interviews with actual residents. I'm grateful to the many people who took the time to tell me about their experiences retiring in Maine. I think you will find that their observations about their community and state, as well as the surprises—both positive and negative—that awaited them as they settled here, add a personal element that mere facts cannot convey.

▲▲▲

Acknowledgments

As I finish writing *Where to Retire in Maine*, I am thankful for all of the people who have helped me in so many ways in its research, writing, and final editing.

First, I am grateful to Neale Sweet and the folks at Down East Books who have been so supportive of my writing career, and would specifically like to thank my editors, Karin Womer and Devon Phillips, for their careful work. I wish to express my appreciation to everyone in the many town offices, libraries, chambers of commerce, and cozy houses across Maine who helped with this book. Specifically, I give sincere thanks to Marilyn Fogg of Cornish, who also helped me with photographs; Peter and Janice Hanson of Kennebunk; Dick and Fran Lalley of Cape Neddick; Margaret Alford of York Harbor; Fred Von Kannewurff of Bridgton; Bill and Betty Haubert of Bridgton (also super photographers!); Jeffrey and Bette Roberts of South Portland; Rhea Freedman of Portland; Kenneth and Marjorie Smith of Brunswick; Charles Murray of Farmington; Bob Silvia of Rangeley; Don Palmer of Rangeley; Halsey and Carol Howe of Boothbay Harbor; Barbara and Ray Ripley of Boothbay Harbor; Anne White of Greene; Charles Peillet of Greene; Imogene and Sam Casey of Belgrade; Meredith and Jay Scheck of Camden; Mike Silverton of Belfast; Mary Lynn Vernon of Dover-Foxcroft; Elizabeth Siegel of Bangor; Liz Knowlton of Blue Hill; Bob and Carol Bonini of Castine; and Warren Craft of Ellsworth.

I wish also to thank all of the very kind people at Maine's retirement communities, as well as the many real estate professionals who shared their thoughts and advice. I enjoyed speaking with the law enforcement officials in each town and appreciate their time and the good work they are doing to keep our state safe.

I owe a debt of gratitude to all of the photographers whose work appears on the following pages. Their images add much to my words, and I am grateful for their creativity and kindness.

And finally, thanks to my husband, Ed, for his encouragement and support, and to my three children, Matt, Nate, and Alexandra, who add immeasurably to my life here in Maine.

The Cornish Inn offers old-fashioned relaxation to visitors to Maine's Southern Gateway. PHOTO COURTESY OF THE CORNISH INN

▲▲▲

Southern Gateway

Cross the Piscataquis River Bridge from New Hampshire, and you've entered Maine's Southern Gateway, occupied by the state's oldest and most southerly county, York. Created in 1652 as "Yorkshire Province," it is best known for its broad beaches of pure white sand and picturesque New England towns. Famous villages such as Wells, Ogunquit, York, and Kennebunkport are etched in generations of vacationers' memories, along with classic lighthouses, rocky shores, and busy lobster pounds. From Kittery in the south to Old Orchard Beach in the north, this part of southern Maine is popular both with vacationers and new Mainers, many of whom commute to Portland or Portsmouth, New Hampshire, for jobs. Little wonder that some of Maine's wealthiest communities are in York County, as well as many of the state's fastest growing towns.

But the Southern Gateway region isn't just about beach towns. The county's northernmost towns are in the foothills of the western mountains, and forest, hills, and farms lining quiet rural roads are the norm. The quiet town of Cornish, located at the very top of York County, offers small-town living, affordability, and proximity to the shopping, cultural, and transportation options of Boston and the rest of southern New England.

York County's neighboring cities Biddeford and Saco (populations 20,942 and 16,822 respectively) together make up the area's largest center of commerce. Inland, the sizeable town of Sanford (population 20,806) is one of the state's fastest growing towns.

The Southern Gateway—both its coastal and inland areas—is a popular place to retire, and there are many desirable communities to choose from. Of the many options, this book profiles York, known for its history and beauty; Kennebunk, home of several top-quality retirement villages; and Cornish, friendly and unspoiled.

Cornish   *York County*

At a Glance

Land Area: 22.09 square miles
Persons per Square Mile: 57.4
Population: 1,269
Median Age: 40.5 years
Neighboring Communities: Baldwin, Parsonsfield, Hiram, Porter

Cornish, located halfway between Portland and New Hampshire's Mount Washington Valley, exudes a friendly, open attitude. Stroll down Main and Maple Streets, where many of the colonial and Victorian homes were moved by teams of oxen to make way for a new stagecoach route in the 1850s, and it feels as if the clock has turned back to when small towns were the norm. A nineteenth-century country inn anchors a downtown full of inviting streets lined with small shops and businesses such as the Cornish Trading Company, a multidealer antiques shop. This quiet York County town is proud of finishing second in a 1997 poll by the *Maine Sunday Telegram* that rated the best small towns in Maine. Of course, there are many folks here who deem Cornish number one!

Cornish was incorporated in 1794. At the local historical society, a dedicated bunch works to preserve the town's past, despite the nearly total loss of documents in long-ago fires. It is known that the area was the sight of some battles during the French and Indian War, and that its original name was Francisborough, then Cornishville. Today, the Cornish Association of Businesses promotes the tranquil setting as "the crown of York County," a somewhat lofty title for a very down-to-earth place.

"The quaint village of Cornish has recently enjoyed a remarkable revitalization," says Paul Howe of DeWolfe Cote & Howe, one of Cornish's few real estate companies. "Antique shops and small businesses, all within easy walking distance, have sprung up in a downtown that takes people back to the way life used to be. Cornish maintains the friendliness of a small community while providing the conveniences of most modern services."

Although this is southern Maine, Cornish is rural. You won't find an automatic car wash, but you can canoe the Great Ossipee and Saco Rivers, which both flow through town. "The living is quiet, away from the city, crime, congestion, and traffic lights," says retiree Marilyn Fogg. "There are apples, blueberries, and vegetables in abundance. All one needs to live in sublimity!"

⚊ WEATHER

Average Temperature (degrees Fahrenheit): January, 15.5; April, 41.4; July, 67.5; October, 44.9. **Average Annual Rainfall:** 37 inches. **Average Annual Snowfall:** 80.1 inches.

⚊ TAXES

Property Tax Rate: $17.05 per $1,000 valuation. **Ratio to Current Market Value:** 90%.

⚊ REAL ESTATE

Provided by Paul Howe, DeWolfe Cote & Howe (207-625-3222)
Older Housing Stock: $100,000 to $300,000, depending on location. **New Custom Construction:** $150,000 and up, depending on size and location. **Waterfront Locations:** $100,000. **Riverfront Lots:** $50,000. **Rental Apartments:** $700/month.

♠ RETIREMENT LIVING

Although there are no real retirement communities here, the Cornish Station Apartments (207-625-3524) as well as a development called Pumpkinville provide housing for the elderly. Call York Cumberland Housing (207-839-6516) for more information.

♠ PUBLIC SAFETY

Troop A of the Maine State Police serves the town of Cornish along with the York County Sheriff's Department. Troop A has twenty-four-hour coverage, and Cornish is one of fifteen towns that receive full law enforcement services.

Non-emergency Police: 207-793-4500. **Non-emergency Fire**: 207-625-3311. **Emergency**: 911.

Lieutenant Ted Short, commanding officer of Troop A of the Maine State Police, says, "We handle, on average, about 300 calls annually in Cornish. I would characterize the town as a quiet rural community with a low crime rate. Troop A is very community oriented,

Bonney Memorial Library, built in 1928. PHOTO BY ERNEST ROSE

and we look to be proactive to provide the best services possible in an attempt to keep towns like Cornish safe places to live, work, and raise a family."

⚲ HEALTH CARE

Closest Hospitals: Goodall Hospital, in Sanford, with 49 acute-care beds, is the closest facility (207-324-4310; www.goodallhospital.org). **Clinics**: Sacopee Valley Health Center, in Porter (207-625-8126).

⚲ CONTINUING EDUCATION

Senior College Program: Closest is in Bridgton, 45 minutes away (207-647-5054). **Colleges and Universities**: Closest is the University of Southern Maine's Gorham campus (800-800-4USM). **Adult Education Programs**: Sacopee Valley High School, in Hiram (207-625-3208).

⚲ LIBRARY

Bonney Memorial Library has provided quality collections, resources, and services to meet and support the educational, informational, and recreational interests of the community since 1928 (207-625-8083; www.bonney.lib.me.us).

⚲ HISTORICAL SOCIETY

Cornish Historical Society (207-625-3280)

⚲ SPECIFICALLY FOR SENIORS

A few programs are provided through York County Community Action (800-644-4202).

⚲ VOLUNTEERING

The Historical Society, located in the front office of Pike Memorial Hall, welcomes new members (207-625-3280).

♠ RECREATION

Golf: Province Lake in Parsonsfield is a semiprivate course (207-795-4040). **Tennis Courts**: Sacopee Valley High School has two public tennis courts. **Parks**: Thompson Park, in the heart of the village, is owned by the town. **Running/Walking/Biking**: A route along the railroad tracks is in the works. **Fitness Classes**: Sanford/Springvale YMCA (207-324-4942). **Hunting/Fishing**: Call the Town Office for licenses at (207-625-4324). **Skiing**: Cross-country skiers use some local snowmobiling trails; groomed trails are found at Five Fields Farm (207-647-2425). Alpine skiers head to Shawnee Peak (207-647-8444; www.shawneepeak.com) for more than forty trails and glades.

♠ ENTERTAINMENT

Cinemas: Closest cinemas are located in Windham, Saco, and North Conway, New Hampshire.

♠ NATURE

Trails up Douglas Hill Mountain in Baldwin are five miles away and lead to fine vistas.

♠ SHOPPING

An IGA supermarket is located on Route 25. The town's Main Street boasts a variety of small stores, including Rosemary's Gift Shop, The Smith Family Antiques, and Mason's Variety Store. The nearest mall is Maine Mall in South Portland, thirty-five miles away.

♠ WHO LIVES HERE

Population: 1,269. **Median Age**: 40.5 years. **Percentage Age 62 and Older**: 19.5%. **Percentage with Bachelor's Degree**: 10.2%. **Percentage with Graduate or Professional Degree**: 5.7%. **Median**

Household Income: $38,125. **Mean Retirement Income**: $14,266.
Per Capita Income: $17,494.

⚑ ESSENTIAL PHONE NUMBERS AND WEB SITES

Chamber of Commerce: Cornish Association of Businesses (207-625-8083; www.cornish-maine.org). **Town Office**: (207-625-4324).
Voter and Vehicle Registration: (207-625-4324). **Drivers' Licenses**:
Can be obtained at the Municipal Building at 55 Washington Street
in Limerick from 10:30 a.m. to 1:30 p.m. on the Monday preceding
every third Tuesday.

⚑ LOCAL NEWS

Newspapers: *Sanford News* (207-324-5986), *Your Weekly Shopping Guide*
(207-625-4334). **Community Cable Station**: Channel 2. **Community
Internet Sites**: www.cornish-maine.org, www.villageprofile.com.

⚑ TRANSPORTATION

Bus: Concord Trailways (800-639-3317) operates a shuttle from Saco
and Biddeford to Portland. **Closest Airport**: Portland International
Jetport (207-774-7301). **Train**: Amtrak in Portland is closest. **Traffic**:
Can be busy during the summer months, due to the town's proximity
to Sebago Lake.

⚑ DISTANCE TO OTHER CITIES

Portland, Me. 33.7 miles
Bangor, Me. 150.8 miles
Boston, Mass. 123.1 miles
New York, N.Y. 327.9 miles
Montreal, Quebec 249.4 miles
Quebec City, Quebec 321.9 miles

⚡ JOBS

Cornish is one of seventeen communities in the Sebago Lakes Region Labor Market. Annual figures for the area in 2001 were: **Civilian Labor Force**: 13,620; **Employed**: 13,100; **Unemployed**: 520; **Unemployment Rate**: 3.8%

⚡ UTILITIES

Electricity: Central Maine Power (800-750-4000). **Water**: Cornish Water District (207-625-8642). **Telephone**: Verizon (800-585-4466). **Cable TV**: Adelphia (800-336-9988). **Internet Service Providers**: Points South (207-490-4949).

> *Cornish is an ideal area for retirees for many reasons, particularly its great location in the foothills of southwestern Maine, forty-five minutes from Portland and the White Mountains area of New Hampshire.*
>
> —Paul Howe,
> DeWolfe Cote & Howe

⚡ PLACES OF WORSHIP

Typical of many New England towns, Cornish's white-steepled Congregational Church on Main Street is the hub of many activities. Churches of other denominations dot the countryside; the closest synagogue is in Portland.

⚡ EVENTS AND FESTIVALS

The Cornish Fairgrounds are the site of an antiques show held each August. The Annual Cornish Apple Festival is held in September in Thompson Park. Attractions include apple products of all kinds, an early-morning pancake breakfast, a 5K run, and a parade of antique cars.

⚡ RESTAURANTS

Two restaurants are right in town: Auntie M's (207-625-3889) and the Thompson Park Grill (207-625-7646).

♠ LODGING

The Cornish Inn offers sixteen rooms, with private bathrooms, and is located on the town's quaint Main Street (800-352-7235; www.cornishinn.com). The Midway Motel (207-625-8835; www.mainemidwaymotel.com) has rooms with cable television and air conditioning.

♠ WHAT THE LOCALS SAY

Marilyn Fogg lived in Maine for sixty-five years before retiring to the Upper Catskill Mountains of New York. After several years, she returned to Maine because she missed "the spaciousness and serenity

---

Bonney Memorial Library

P.O. Box 857
36 Main Street, Cornish

Hours:
Monday and Wednesday, 10:30 a.m. to 12:30 p.m.; 3:00 to 7:00 p.m.
Tuesday and Thursday, 1:00 to 6:00 p.m.
Saturday, 10:30 a.m. to 12:30 p.m. (except July and August)

Bonney Memorial Library was built in 1928 by Dr. Sherman Bonney in memory of his parents, Dr. Calvin and Mrs. Harriet Bonney. Dr. Bonney closed the library dedication with: "...Let its doors be open to all who care to read and learn." The library provides a variety of materials, services, and programs: fiction and nonfiction books, audiocassettes, large-print books, magazines, videos, computers with Internet access, interlibrary loan, and special programs. At www.bonney.lib.me.us, one can find information on library events and programs, view the latest edition of the library's *Bookworm News* newsletter, see a list of the newest acquisitions, and more.

---

of the Maine countryside" as well as family and lifelong friends. When she made the trek back to the Pine Tree State, it was to Cornish that Marilyn gravitated, buying a home and settling in year-round.

"Cornish is equipped with all the amenities to satisfy a retiree," she says. "There are the library, pharmacy, grocery store, hardware store, and well-trained fire and ambulance services. Near and in the village are restaurants, gas stations, the post office, garden supply stores, and, of course, the video store!"

Marilyn became involved in a local church and quickly forged new friendships. Despite the fact that generations of the same families live here, "It's easy to get connected in a small town," she says.

Before moving to Cornish, Marilyn was apprehensive about its remoteness. "Travel to the city—especially for health reasons—was a concern. It is forty-five minutes to Portland's hospitals, but there is an excellent rescue-and-ambulance service here, and we are connected with 911." While she loves the serenity of this corner of York County, she concedes that the Cornish lifestyle may not be right for everyone. "Some retirees have special needs beyond what the local doctor and clinic can satisfy," she notes. And while she advises those thinking of relocating here to "make the move now," she does add: "I have yet to find someone who plays bridge."

Kennebunk *York County*

At a Glance

Land Area: 35 square miles
Persons per Square Mile: 299
Population: 10,476
Median Age: 41.3 years
Neighboring Communities: Arundel, Kennebunkport, Wells, and Biddeford

The town of Kennebunk lies on Maine's southern coast, nestled between the Mousam and Kennebunk Rivers. It's a place with many distinct neighborhoods and nearly as many names. Downtown, tree-lined streets showcase eighteenth- and nineteenth-century architecture, the legacy of prosperous merchants and sea captains who once called the area home. Along with the famous Victorian "Wedding Cake House," with its icing-like adornment, are fine examples of Greek Revival, colonial, and Federal-style structures. Toward the coast, the part of town known as Kennebunk Beach—actually three wide and welcoming stretches of sand—beckons to those who love waves and water. Along the Kennebunk River lies the Lower Village, a commercial area also known as Kennebunk Landing. And finally, head toward the sunset (west of both the old "Portland Road" and Interstate 95), and you'll find yourself in yet another section of the community: West Kennebunk.

If all this seems just a bit confusing, hang on, because Kennebunk's close neighbor is the village of Kennebunk*port*. It's a bustling place, best known as the summer home of former President George Bush and his wife, Barbara. Within "the Port's" town lines are Cape

Porpoise, a typical working harbor, and Goose Rocks, a tiny village with a long sweep of wide beach. Just to the north is the town of Arundel,

*Kennebunk's famous
"Wedding Cake House."*
PHOTO COURTESY OF THE
KENNEBUNK CHAMBER OF
COMMERCE

33

home of the renowned Arundel Barn Playhouse. Things can get tricky with all these names floating about, so locals solve the problem by skipping the technicalities and calling the whole lot "the Kennebunks." It's a much easier way to refer to several seaside villages that have been important fixtures of the southern coast since the 1620s.

Although the Kennebunks were originally settled for their rich fishing grounds, the area became a haven for tourists in the mid-1800s, when scores of sprawling seaside hotels and rambling shingled "cottages" dotted the shoreline. Today, tourism is still big business, thanks to the area's spectacular five-mile coast, complete with sandy beaches, rocky vistas, and traditional waterfront activities. Adding to the inherent scenic beauty are amenities such as restaurants, theaters, golf courses, and a good variety of specialty shops. Given the mix of cultural and recreational opportunities available here, it's no wonder that the Kennebunks are a bustling destination for thousands of visitors each summer and fall, as well as a growing number of winter guests, who bundle up for Kennebunkport's annual Christmas Prelude.

Retirement in the Kennebunks means enjoying all that this corner of Maine has to offer on a year-round basis: watching the lupines bloom brightly along the shore of Cape Porpoise; strolling Gooch's Beach to Lord's Point; gliding on the cross-country trails through snowy Lafayette Park. Walk the streets of downtown, and you feel a strong sense of community pride, as evidenced by the town's well-loved public library and the district's nationally acclaimed school system. These attributes, plus the availability of excellent medical care and new retirement communities, combined with the area's proximity to Boston and Portland, have made this part of York County extremely popular with retirees. "We haven't found a downside to living in Kennebunk," say newcomers Peter and Janice Hanson. "The taxes are high, but it's worth paying them for the privilege of living in such a vibrant community."

▲ WEATHER

Average Temperature (degrees Fahrenheit): January, 21.6; April, 41.9; July, 66.7; October, 46.9. **Average Annual Rainfall:** 43 inches. **Average Annual Snowfall:** 71 inches.

▲ TAXES

Property Tax Rate: $21.04 per $1,000 valuation. **Ratio to Current Market Value:** 95%.

▲ REAL ESTATE

Provided by John D. Downing, Downing Real Estate (207-985-3328)
Older Housing Stock: $150,000 to $1,000,000, depending on location. **New Custom Construction:** $175,000 and up, depending on size and location. **Waterfront Locations:** None available at this writing. **Riverfront Lots:** $175,000. **Rental Apartments:** $1,000/month.

▲ RETIREMENT LIVING

The Farragut (877-985-0300; www.thefarragut.com) is within walking distance of town and offers single-level and cottage-style homes as well as an inn with common rooms, indoor pool, fitness center, library, and café. Huntington Common (800-585-0533; www.huntingtoncommon.com) offers independent apartments, cottages, assisted living units, and a memory impairment area along the Kennebunk River.

> *Kennebunk is desirable for many reasons, but mainly because we offer lots of things for retirees to do and are an easy trip away from Portland and Boston.*
>
> —John D. Downing,
> Downing Agency Real Estate

▲ PUBLIC SAFETY

Crimes per 1,000 Population, 2000: 18.81. **Non-emergency Police:** 207-985-6121. **Non-emergency Fire:** 207-985-7113. **Emergency:** 911.

Mathew Baker, Kennebunk's chief of police, describes his town as "a nice community, with relatively low crime. It's a very safe place overall." The Maine Department of Public Safety bears out his assessment: in 2000, only 179 crimes were reported in Kennebunk, none of them homicides.

⚡ HEALTH CARE

Closest Hospitals: Southern Maine Medical Center (SMMC), a 150-bed acute-care community hospital, is located ten minutes away in Biddeford. The hospital provides a full range of inpatient and out-

---

Kennebunk Free Library
112 Main Street, Kennebunk

Hours:
Monday and Tuesday, 9:30 a.m. to 8:00 p.m.
Wednesday, 12:30 p.m. to 8:00 p.m.
Thursday, 9:30 a.m to 5:00 p.m.
Friday and Saturday, 9:30 a.m. to 5:00 p.m.
Saturday (July/August only), 10:00 a.m. to 1:00 p.m.

Kennebunk Free Library has strived to meet the educational and recreational needs of the town of Kennebunk and its surrounding communities since 1882. Building projects in 1907 and 1995 have given the town the beautiful structure that stands today. The library's collection of more than 37,000 volumes includes videos, audios, large-print books, a Maine collection, and the Bolton Travel Collection. The staff provides reference services in person, by phone, or via e-mail; interlibrary loan, Internet access, and Hank's Room, a community meeting room complete with VCR, TV, and kitchenette. More information can be found at www.kennebunk.me.lib.us.

---

patient services, including medical, surgical, obstetric, pediatric, and mental health. SMMC also has a facility in Kennebunk known as SMMC at Park Square (207- 467-6999), which offers diagnostic testing and therapeutic treatments. **Clinics**: Nearby is the Wells Regional Medical Community (207-646-5211), a service of York Hospital, in Wells, which offers convenient walk-in medical services, laboratory services, radiology, oncology, special procedures, specialty physician offices, and Wells Emergency Medical Services. Kennebunk also has a walk-in clinic, Kennebunk Medical Center (207-985-3726). **Long-term Care Facilities**: Kennebunk Nursing and Rehabilitation Center (207-985-7141), Atria Assisted Living (207-985-5866; www.atriacom.com).

⚑ CONTINUING EDUCATION
Senior College: York County Senior College, located at the University of Sanford and Saco (800-696-3075). **Colleges and Universities**: University of New England (207-283-0171), York County Technical College (207-646-9282), Heartwood College of Art (207-985-6333). **Adult Education Programs**: Kennebunk Adult Education (207-985-1116). **Elderhostel**: Brick Store Museum (207-985-4802).

⚑ LIBRARY
Kennebunk Free Library (207-985-217; www.kennebunk.lib.me.us)

⚑ HISTORICAL SOCIETY
Kennebunkport Historical Society (207-967-2751)

⚑ SPECIFICALLY FOR SENIORS
The Senior Center at Lower Village (207-967-8514) offers a wide range of activities, including a monthly luncheon, trips, discussion groups, lectures, knitting circles, performing arts sessions, demonstrations, and book clubs.

♠ VOLUNTEERING

"The area has many, many opportunities for volunteer involvement," says newcomer Ted Trainer, who has become active in Rotary, church, and town committees. The Chamber of Commerce is happy to put newcomers in touch with organizations needing help. Some of the many local nonprofits that welcome volunteers are: The Animal Welfare Society, Community Partners, United Way of York County, River Tree Arts, Kennebunk Land Trust, Senior Center at Lower Village, and the Northern York County YMCA.

♠ RECREATION

Golf: Cape Arundel Golf Club (207-967-3494) is a semiprivate course offering morning and afternoon nonmember tee times. The Links at Outlook, in South Berwick, is an eighteen-hole championship public course (207-384-4653; www.Outlookgolf.com). **Tennis Courts**: Kennebunk High School, Parsons Field, Holland Road, and Beachwood Avenue in Kennebunkport. **Parks**: There are several in Kennebunk, including Rotary and Lafayette Parks. **Running/Walking/Biking**: The area offers many in-town as well as beach walking and biking routes. In addition, there are several guided

Lounging on the sand in Kennebunk Beach.

tours, including Architectural Walking Tours (207-985-4802).
Fitness Classes: Kennebunk Health & Fitness Center (207-985-1234),
Fitness Nut House (207-985-7727), Northern York County YMCA
(207-283-0100). **Horses/Riding**: Bush Brook Stables (207-284-7721).
Hunting/Fishing: Call the Town Office for licenses at (207-985-2102).
Several guided sportfishing services offer saltwater fishing, such as
Lady J Sportfishing Charters (207-985-7304) and Stone Coast Anglers
(207-985-6005). **Skiing**: Cross-country trails are found at Wells
Reserve at Laudholm Farm (207-646-1555); closest downhill area is
Shawnee Peak (207-647-8444).

⚓ ENTERTAINMENT

Cinemas: Flagship Cinema in Wells, Cinemas 8 in Biddeford.
Museums: Brick Store Museum (207-985-4802), Seashore Trolley
Museum (207-967-2712). **Theaters**: Arundel Barn Playhouse (207-
985-5552), Prelude Productions (207-985-7534), River Tree Arts
(207-985-4343).

⚓ NATURE

The Kennebunk Plains offer 1,100 acres of protected grasslands
habitat, ideal for birdwatching or hiking (207-490-4012). In nearby
Wells is the Wells Reserve at Laudholm Farm (207-646-1555), with
1,600 acres of salt marsh, sand dunes, and grassy uplands, as well as
the Rachel Carson National Wildlife Refuge (207-646-9226), featuring an accessible one-mile, self-guided trail.

⚓ SHOPPING

Supermarkets are located in Kennebunk as well as in nearby Wells
and Biddeford. Discount stores are eight to eleven miles away. The
nearest mall is the Maine Mall in South Portland, about thirty miles.
A number of small specialty stores are located in Kennebunk, offering everything from books to jewelry to fishing supplies.

Boats of all sizes visit the Kennebunks.

PHOTO COURTESY OF THE
KENNEBUNK CHAMBER OF COMMERCE

⚓ WHO LIVES HERE

Population: 10,476. Median Age: 41.3 years. Percentage Age 62 and Older: 19.7%. Percentage with Bachelor's Degree: 25.9%. Percentage with Graduate or Professional Degree: 17%. Median Household Income: $49,015. Mean Retirement Income: $14,807. Per Capita Income: $26,562.

⚓ ESSENTIAL PHONE NUMBERS AND WEB SITES

Chamber of Commerce: 207-967-0857; www.visitthekennebunks.com. Town Office: 207-985-2102, www.kennebunk.maine.org. Voter and Vehicle Registration: Town Clerk's Department (207-985-3675). Drivers' Licenses: Motor Vehicle Office (207-985-4890). Newcomers Organization: Kennebunk Newcomer's Club (207-985-8733; www.angelfire.com/me3/kbunknewcomers).

⚓ LOCAL NEWS

Newspapers: *York County Coast Star* (207-985-2961; www.coaststar .com), *Journal Tribune* (207-282-1535; www.journaltribune.com), *Tourist News* (207-985-2244). Community Cable Station: Channel 9.

40

⬆ TRANSPORTATION

Bus: Closest service is in Portland. **Taxi**: Front Line Taxi (866-490-1214), John's Coastal Taxi (207-985-6291). **Tours**: Intown Trolley (207-967-3686). **Closest Airport**: Portland International Jetport (thirty miles). **Limo Service**: Lilley's Limousine (888-546-6765), Mermaid Transportation Co. (207-772-2509). **Train**: Amtrak to Boston's South Station, from Wells. **Traffic**: Usually light; moderate in season.

⬆ DISTANCE TO OTHER CITIES

Portland, Me. 27 miles
Bangor, Me. 160 miles
Boston, Mass. 89 miles
New York, N.Y. 292 miles
Montreal, Quebec 318 miles
Quebec City, Quebec 309 miles

⬆ JOBS

Kennebunk is one of nine communities in the Biddeford Labor Market. Annual figures for the area in 2001 were: **Civilian Labor Force**: 42,130; **Employed**: 40,840; **Unemployed**: 1,290; **Unemployment Rate**: 3.1%

⬆ UTILITIES

Electricity: Central Maine Power (800-750-4000), Kennebunk Light and Power (207-985-3311). **Water**: Kennebunk, Kennebunkport & Wells Water District (207-985-3385). **Sewer**: Kennebunk Sewer District (207-985-4741). **Telephone**: Verizon (800-585-4466). **Cable TV**: Adelphia Media Services (207-967-5271). **Internet Service Providers**: Adelphia Media Services (207-967-5271), Log On America (888-985-3668).

▲ PLACES OF WORSHIP

The Kennebunks offer twenty-one places to worship, including Protestant, Catholic, and interdenominational churches and a Franciscan monastery located on Beach Avenue. The closest synagogues are in Portland; contact the Jewish Federation (207-773-7254) for more information.

▲ EVENTS AND FESTIVALS

Numerous festivals take place throughout the year, including the Annual Home, Food & Craft Show (March), the Blessing of the Fleet (June), Picnic and Concert on the Green (July), Kidfest (September), and Christmas Prelude (December).

▲ RESTAURANTS

Dining choices vary from ethnic fare to traditional seafood. Here are a few options right in Kennebunk: Grissini Trattoria (207-967-2211), The Kennebunk Inn (207- 985-3351), Riverside Grill (207-967-9961).

▲ LODGING

There are dozens of places to stay in the Kennebunks. Be sure to book ahead at these or any other lodging places, especially during the summer. Spofford Inn (207-985-6558; www.spoffordinn.com), Waldo Emerson Inn (207-985-4250; www.bbhoset.com/waldoemersoninn), The Seasons Inn (800-336-5634).

▲ WHAT THE LOCALS SAY

When Peter and Janice Hanson moved to Kennebunk from Wisconsin in 1998, they weren't exactly strangers to the Pine Tree State. Peter cherishes memories of childhood summers spent on Raymond Pond and college years at Bowdoin College in Brunswick, and both Peter and Janice had visited friends and family here. Although the couple was eager to relocate, they postponed the move for several years. "We knew we wanted to come to Maine as soon as we could," explains Janice. "However, we also knew that we had to wait for Peter to retire first. We needed to have a good, stable income before moving here." Looking back, they feel they made the right decision. "When we came to Maine, we were under the impression that taxes would be lower here than they were in Wisconsin, which has the highest tax rate in the country. We soon found that Maine's tax rate is a close second. Living in this state is expensive."

High taxes aside, the Hansons are thrilled with their retirement location. "Local friends gave us the grand tour of the Kennebunks, and we fell in love with this area," says Janice. "We were utterly delighted to find the cultural life of this community and the surrounding communities and Portland to be so excellent that we rarely go to Boston. Before moving here, we thought we would be going south quite often for plays, concerts, museums, and the like. Instead, we stay here, or we head north to Portland.

"The biggest advantages to living in Kennebunk as retirees are: first, getting to know the people who live here. Everyone we've met loves Maine and appreciates what the state has to offer culturally, recreationally, and socially. Next, honesty and integrity are so ingrained in the Maine way of life that everyone expects to be treated fairly, and is. Third, independence in thinking is a refreshing attribute of the Maine character. And finally, there is beauty everywhere. Maine is a place where the soul can blossom."

▲▲▲

York

York County

At a Glance

Land Area: 54.9 square miles
Persons per Square Mile: 234
Population: 12,854
Median Age: 43.4 years
Neighboring Communities: South Berwick, Eliot, Kittery, Ogunquit

As any member of the York Historical Society will tell you, there's a lot of history here. The area was once home to the Native American village of Agamenticus (now the name of a local mountain) that was decimated by a plague in 1616. Two decades later, the first English colonists arrived, and in 1642 their settlement, Gorgeana, became America's first chartered city. Ten years later, Gorgeana was demoted to a town and given a new name, York, in honor of a Puritan victory in the English Civil War. Because Maine was then part of Massachusetts, York was a frontier outpost of the Bay State. For the next 168 years, York bore the burden of continual fighting between the English settlers and the French in Canada and their Indian allies. Although the town suffered numerous raids (including one in which the Congregational minister was killed and 100 residents were taken captive), the site was never abandoned.

A spirit of tenacity—along with a well-preserved historical district composed of seven impeccably restored museum buildings—lives on in York. Despite its popularity (*Money* magazine recently rated York a premier vacation spot due to its beauty, safety, and family appeal) and pricey real estate (York is actually the third highest valued community in all of Maine, ranking below only Portland and South Portland), the town hangs onto its small-town character in much the same way it clings to its colonial roots. Residents are proud of the new public library as well as the area's fine schools and state-of-the-art

York Hospital. The town supports a very active Senior Center, which organizes programs on tax bills as well as jaunts to New York City. Volunteerism is important and valued: those who give of their time are recognized at an annual banquet.

Although technically one unified town, York is better described as "the Yorks," a collection of several little, once-autonomous villages. In addition to York Village, also called Old York, there's York Harbor, York Beach, and Cape Neddick. Each has its own distinct flavor and characteristics.

The most genteel of the villages is York Harbor, a tony community near the mouth of the York River where yachts bob at anchor, awaiting their owners. York Village lies along the banks of the river, and at its center is the Old York Historical Society, site of the town's living-history quarter. Seven historic museum buildings, including the Old Gaol (jail), the earliest example of stone architecture in the United States, line the main street. From June through Columbus Day, the area bustles with ice cream cone–licking tourists, who throng the sidewalks to get a feel for colonial times. Meanwhile, just to the north, Short Sands Beach, Long Sands Beach, and Nubble Lighthouse, all parts of York Beach, buzz with activity as well. Even farther north is Cape Neddick, a slightly calmer, more residential part of the Yorks.

> *There are many benefits to living in York—from the charm and history of a small seacoast community with typical New England architecture to the tempering effects of the ocean on both our winters and our summers.*
>
> —Ginny Whitney, Anne Erwin Real Estate

Despite their differences, all of these communities call themselves York, and all celebrated in the town's 350th anniversary, marked in 2002 with a yearlong celebration of pride and community spirit.

Close to both the sea and the rest of New England, York has grown significantly in recent decades. Both the Maine Turnpike and U.S. Route 1 cut through York, making for easy access to Portsmouth, New Hampshire and Boston, Massachusetts. Acclaimed schools and hospitals are nearby. And then there's the tangible pull of the past. York Police Chief David Bracy sums it up nicely by saying, "The town is steeped in colonial history yet provides many of the twenty-first century amenities that make living here a unique dream."

⚑ WEATHER
Average Temperature (degrees Fahrenheit): January, 21.6; April, 41.9; July, 66.7; October, 46.9. **Average Annual Rainfall:** 34 inches. **Average Annual Snowfall:** 69 inches.

⚑ TAXES
Property Tax Rate: $10.25 per $1,000 valuation. **Ratio to Current Market Value:** 100%.

Twenty-one single-story cottages fill the grounds at Sentry Hill, in York.

♦ REAL ESTATE

Provided by Ginny Whitney, Anne Erwin Real Estate (207-363-6640)
Older Housing Stock: $130,000 to $3,000,000 (average price, $370,485), depending on location. **New Custom Construction**: $250,000 and up, depending on size and location. **Waterfront Locations**: $250,000 to $3,000,000 (average price, $959,741). **Riverfront Lots**: $295,000 to $320,000 (only two available at this writing). **Rental Apartments**: $750/month.

♦ RETIREMENT LIVING

Sentry Hill, built in 1998, offers independent apartments, cottage units, assisted living, long-term care, and an Alzheimer's unit for 160 residents (207-363-5116; www.sentryhill.com). Spring Pond Estates (207-363-3975; www.springpondestates.com) has 32 cottage units, which were constructed in 1999.

♦ PUBLIC SAFETY

Crimes per 1,000 Population, 2000: 18.71. **Non-emergency Police**: 207-363-1031. **Non-emergency Fire**: 207-363-1015. **Emergency**: 911.

Douglas Bracy, chief of police, describes his town as "a picturesque coastal community whose beauty is only surpassed by the quality of life it has to offer. I am proud to be a part of the public safety network that provides full-time fire, police, and paramedic services."

♦ HEALTH CARE

Closest Hospitals: York Hospital (207-363-4321), described as "Maine's Most Caring Hospital" by *Down East* magazine, provides medical/surgical units, twenty-four-hour emergency services, extensive inpatient and outpatient services, and many year-round community programs. **Clinics**: At York Hospital. **Long-Term Care Facilities**: Sentry Hill (207-363-5116; www.sentryhill.com).

↟ CONTINUING EDUCATION

Senior College: York County Senior College, located at the University of Sanford and Saco (1-800-696-3075). **Colleges and Universities**: Closest is in Wells, York County Technical College (207-646-9282). **Adult Education Programs**: York High School Adult Education (207-363-7922).

↟ LIBRARY

York Public Library (207-363-2818; www.york.lib.me.us).

↟ HISTORICAL SOCIETY

The Old York Historical Society was founded 100 years ago and features thirty-seven period room settings throughout seven buildings. (207-363-4974; www.oldyork.org).

York Public Library
15 Long Sands Road, York

Hours:
Wednesday, 12:00 noon to 8:00 p.m.
Thursday and Friday, 10:00 a.m. to 5:00 p.m.
Saturday, 10:00 a.m. to 2:00 p.m.

York Public Library, built in 2001, is in the middle of the village, and offers free Internet access, photocopies, interlibrary loan, reference help in person and on the telephone, renewals by telephone and over the Internet, and free delivery of books to shut-ins. The collection numbers 43,655 items. The library has a reciprocal agreement with libraries in Ogunquit and Wells, and cardholders in those towns may visit all three libraries. For more information, see www.york.me.lib.us.

⚑ SPECIFICALLY FOR SENIORS

York Senior Citizens Center (207-363-1036) is very active, holding classes, luncheons, and an annual health fair in August.

The Old Gaol, one of seven buildings owned by the Old York Historical Society.
Below, the beautifully restored Jefferd's Tavern.

PHOTOS COURTESY OF THE OLD YORK HISTORICAL SOCIETY

♠ VOLUNTEERING

Friends of the York Public Library (207-363-2818) welcomes new members, as do the Old York Historical Society (207-363-4974) and York Community Service Association (207-363-5504).

♠ RECREATION

Golf: Ledges Golf Course (207-351-3000) is a championship eighteen-hole, par seventy-two course. The Links at Outlook in nearby South Berwick (207-384-4653) is also eighteen holes. York Golf & Tennis Club (207-363-0130) offers challenging play as well. **Tennis Courts**: At York High School, also York Golf & Tennis Club (207-363-0130). **Parks**: Ellis Park with its gazebo at Short Sands Beach. **Running/Walking**: Stroll the beaches or climb 691-foot-high Mount Agamenticus's trails. **Fitness Classes**: Curves for Women (207-363-9637). **Hunting/Fishing**: Mainely Fishing (207-363-6526); call the Town Office for licenses at (207-363-1003). **Skiing**: Cross-country skiers enjoy local golf courses; closest downhill area is Loon Mountain in New Hampshire. **Garden Club**: 207-363-2787.

♠ ENTERTAINMENT

Cinemas: Leavitt Theatre (207-646-3123). **Museums**: Old York Historical Society (207-363-4974; www.oldyork.org); Ogunquit Museum of American Art (207-646-4909). **Theaters**: In nearby Berwick is the Hackmatack Playhouse (207-698-1807; www.hackmatack.org), in Ogunquit is the Playhouse (207-646-2402; www.ogunquitplayhouse.org), and in Portsmouth is Seacoast Repertory Theatre (603-433-4793; www.seacoastrep.org).

♠ NATURE

The York Land Trust (207 363-7400; www.yorklandtrust.org) was founded in 1986 by a group of concerned citizens and has several properties suitable for nature study. In nearby Wells is the Wells

Reserve at Laudholm Farm (207-646-1555), with 1,600 acres of salt marsh, sand dunes, and grassy uplands, as well as the Rachel Carson National Wildlife Refuge (207-646-9226), featuring an accessible one-mile, self-guided trail.

▲ SHOPPING

Several supermarkets are located right in York. The nearest mall is across the bridge in Portsmouth, New Hampshire. Dozens of outlet stores are found in Kittery, about six miles away.

▲ WHO LIVES HERE

Population: 12,854. **Median Age**: 43.4. **Percentage Age 62 and Older**: 20.3%. **Percentage with Bachelor's Degree**: 26.7%. **Percentage with Graduate or Professional Degree**: 10.9%. **Median Household Income**: $56,171. **Mean Retirement Income**: $22,276. **Per Capita Income**: $30,895.

▲ ESSENTIAL PHONE NUMBERS AND WEB SITES

Chamber of Commerce: 207-363-4422; www.info@yorkme.org. **Town Office**: 207-363-1003, www.yorkmaine.org. **Voter and Vehicle Registration**: Town Clerk's Department (207-363-1003). **Drivers' Licenses**: Motor Vehicle Office (207-985-4890).

▲ LOCAL NEWS

Newspapers: *The York Independent* (207-363-2600), *York County Coast Star* (207-985-2961), *The York Weekly* (207-363-4343; www.yorkweekly .maine.com). **Community Cable Station**: Channel 3. **Community Internet Sites**: www.yorkmaine.org.

▲ TRANSPORTATION

Bus: Closest stop is at Pease Air Force Base in New Hampshire. **Closest Airport**: Pease Airport in Portsmouth, New Hampshire.

Taxi: Frontline Taxi (207-646-7766). **Train**: Amtrak is accessible in Wells. **Traffic**: Can be busy in summer months, especially on weekends.

▲ DISTANCE TO OTHER CITIES

Portland, Me. 45.2 miles

Bangor, Me. 173.4 miles

Boston, Mass. 71 miles

New York, N.Y. 275.8 miles

Montreal, Quebec 302.9 miles

Quebec City, Quebec 313.2 miles

▲ JOBS

York is one of five communities in the Kittery–York Labor Market. Annual figures for the area in 2001 were: **Civilian Labor Force**: 21,050; **Employed**: 20,540; **Unemployed**: 520; **Unemployment Rate**: 2.5%

▲ UTILITIES

Electricity: Central Maine Power (800-750-4000). **Water**: York Water District (207-363-2265). **Sewer**: 207-363-4232. **Telephone**: Verizon (800-585-4466). **Cable TV**: Adelphia (800-336-9988). **Internet Service Providers**: Great Works Internet (800-201-1476, www.gwi.net).

▲ PLACES OF WORSHIP

As befits an old New England town, York contains quite a few white-steepled churches, including Union Congregational Church (appropriately located on Church Street) and the First Parish Church, which has its roots in the early 1630s. The closest synagogue is in Portsmouth, New Hampshire.

▲ EVENTS AND FESTIVALS

Numerous festivals take place throughout the year, including York Days (end of July), York Beach Treasure Hunt (mid-September) and Harvestfest, a colonial celebration that occurs in October.

▲ RESTAURANTS

Dining choices vary from lobster (Fox's Lobster House, 207-363-2643) to linguine (Fazio's Italian Restaurant, 207-351-3378) to everything in between (Stage Neck Inn, 207-363-3850).

▲ LODGING

The York area is home to more lodging places than perhaps anywhere in Maine. A few to try include the Lynwood Inn (800-852-8410), Golden Pineapple B&B (207-363-7837), and Inn at Harmon Park (207-363-2031).

▲ WHAT THE LOCALS SAY

"We fell in love with this town, its history, and its people," says Dick Lalley, who retired to York in 1995 with his wife, Fran. After spending a few short vacations in the area, the Lalleys packed up their New Hampshire home and bought a small house in Cape Neddick. "We appreciate the convenience of Route 95," says Dick, "and it is a real plus to have York Hospital right here."

Dick and Fran list many advantages to living in York: the natural beauty of the beaches, the high quality of area restaurants, and the welcoming attitude of local residents. "Our town offices are the friendliest in the world," Dick believes. Although another retiree to York says that to come into this town "unconnected" could be difficult, the Lalleys, who moved here without any connections, haven't found this to be true. "We belong to a very active church here," says Dick. "We've found it extremely easy to get involved."

Anyone considering retirement in Maine should come with an open attitude, advises Dick. "Enjoy Maine—don't try to change it." While he has a few minor complaints about the way the state functions ("The income tax is outrageous! We had none in New Hampshire"), he has no regrets about moving to York. "I wish I had come here sooner," he says.

▲▲▲

Greater
Portland

Anchored by the city of Portland, the largest
metropolitan area north of Boston, as well as its suburbs,
the Greater Portland region is the state's most populous area.
Here are the Cumberland County towns of Scarborough, Yarmouth,
and Falmouth, as well as Windham, Westbrook, and South Portland.
Farther up the coast are Freeport, home of renowned sporting goods
retailer L.L. Bean as well as numerous "outlet" stores, restaurants, inns,
and 7,400 residents. Brunswick, a town of more than 21,000 people,
is the site of historic Bowdoin College as well as Brunswick Naval
Air Station.

Inland, Cumberland County's Sebago Lake is the second largest
in Maine and the source of much of southern Maine's drinking water.
Ringed with camps, motels, and resorts, Sebago is enjoyed year-round
by residents of the neighboring towns of Windham, Raymond, Naples,
Bridgton, and Standish.

Greater Portland is a busy, prosperous part of Maine, containing the state's largest mall, largest hospital, and largest airport. And
yet this section of the state also offers craggy seaside cliffs, quiet
tidal marshes, clean lakes, and tranquil islands.

In fact, many Cumberland County towns offer exactly what so
many retirees want: safe neighborhoods, scenic beauty, good services,
and friendly residents. While it was difficult to decide which communities to include, I decided on Portland, South Portland, Brunswick,
and Bridgton.

Naturally, the city of Portland is a draw for the retiree who
longs for cultural activities, historic neighborhoods, and small-town
charm. Just across the bridge is South Portland, a community in its

55

own right, offering slightly more affordable housing as well as proximity to health care and shopping. Farther north in Cumberland County is Brunswick, designated a town but as large and vibrant as a small city. Brunswick is a perennial favorite with new Mainers who enjoy its diversity, thriving downtown, and lively arts scene. Finally, the little lakeside community of Bridgton offers beautiful scenery, old-fashioned neighborliness, and recreational opportunities all year long.

Bridgton   *Cumberland County*

At a Glance

Land Area: 50.51 square miles
Persons per Square Mile: 97.6
Population: 4,883
Median Age: 39.8 years
Neighboring Communities: Naples, Harrison, Denmark, Fryeburg, Sebago

There is a timeless tranquility to Bridgton, a small town that bills itself as the gateway to Maine's western lakes and mountains. Walk down the main thoroughfare, and you're more likely to spot bicycles than BMWs, denim than designer duds. Mom-and-pop and antiques stores line the downtown streets, while canoes ply the area's many lakes. The crunch of snow signals the start of the quietest season here, and the cries of loons herald the return of spring.

"Bridgton is a town that has progressed into the twenty-first century but has not forgotten the values of community, friendship, and brotherhood," says Western Maine Realtor of the Year for 2002 Tim Perry. Retirees here enjoy the area's four-season activities, mainly centered on the great outdoors, as well as its convenient proximity to medical care and surprisingly wide array of educational opportunities for seniors.

The village of Bridgton sits astride Route 302, which runs from Portland north and west to New Hampshire. The town itself is composed of several areas: North Bridgton, at the top of Long Lake; West Bridgton, by the shores of Moose Pond; and South Bridgton, also called Sandy Creek. Although the town borders busy Naples and Sebago Lake, much of Bridgton operates at a slower pace, even in summer. Along with the town's large lakes and numerous ponds are several mountains, including Pleasant Mountain, better known to skiers as Shawnee Peak.

Along with the pleasant scenery and laid-back lifestyle, what draws retirees to this area is the welcoming nature of the community. "This is a town that really values its seniors," says Dona Forke, executive director of the Bridgton Community Center. Housed at the Community Center is Horizons/60, a dynamic program for retirement-aged residents of the lakes towns. The initiative began with a community development grant but now receives funding from the town. Participants take courses and trips, listen to luncheon talks, and use the center's computers and complete resource library. Dona Forke says the town is committed to its older residents and is now seeking grants to establish a senior transportation system. Along with Horizons/60, area seniors can attend Bridgton's Senior College, located in the Memorial School building next door to the Community Center. These programs, along with various volunteer opportunities and activities held at the high school and Bridgton Academy, mean retirees here never lack for things to do.

"Our seniors are the busiest people I know," says Carmen Lone of the Greater Bridgton Lakes Region Chamber of Commerce. "They're taking classes, they're volunteering, and they're outside enjoying nature. It's a wonderful community for them."

⚐ WEATHER

Average Temperature (degrees Fahrenheit): January, 16.5; April, 41.3; July, 67.2; October, 45.5. **Average Annual Rainfall**: 45.37 inches. **Average Annual Snowfall**: 80.1 inches

> *Bridgton is a town where it is still fun to walk the main street, window shop, meet old friends, and just enjoy the clean, fresh air.*
>
> —Tim Perry,
> RE/MAX at the Lakes

⚐ TAXES

Property Tax Rate: $17.90 per $1,000 valuation. **Ratio to Current Market Value**: 100%.

⚐ REAL ESTATE

Provided by Tim Perry, RE/MAX at The Lakes (207-583-6211)

Older Housing Stock: $89,000 to $925,000, depending on location. **New Custom Construction**: $200,000 and up, depending on size and location. **Waterfront Locations**: $350,000 and up. **Water Access**: $99,000 and up. **Riverfront Lots**: $20,000. **Rental Apartments**: $550/month.

⚐ RETIREMENT LIVING

Bridgton has no retirement communities.

⚐ PUBLIC SAFETY

Crimes per 1,000 Population, 2000: 50.51. **Non-emergency Police**: 207-647-8814. **Non-emergency Fire**: 207-647-8814. **Emergency**: 911.

"This is an exceptional community," says Robert Bell, Bridgton's chief of police. "Many retirees relocate here, especially summer people who have been coming up for years." He points out that although his department receives a number of service calls— mainly for thefts of skis at Shawnee Peak and speeding—serious crime is low in Bridgton. "It's a place I would characterize as very safe," he says.

The interior of newly renovated Bridgton Hospital is bright and cheerful.
PHOTO BY PAMELA SMITH

▲ HEALTH CARE

Closest Hospitals: Newly renovated Bridgton Hospital (207-647-8841; www.bridgtonhospital.org) has 21 private rooms. **Clinics**: Bridgton Hospital has a dedicated 24-hour emergency wing. **Long-Term Care Facilities**: Bridgton Health Care Center (207-647-8821). **Home Health Care**: Community Health Services (800-479-4331); Androscoggin Home Care & Hospice (800-847-0008).

▲ CONTINUING EDUCATION

Senior College: Bridgton Senior College (208-647-5054). **Colleges and Universities**: Southern Maine Technical College (207-647-5054). **Adult Education Programs**: Everything from bread making to bird-watching and more (208-647-5054).

▲ LIBRARY

Bridgton Public Library (207-647-2472; www.bridgton.lib.me.us).

▲ HISTORICAL SOCIETY

An active group publishes a newsletter and holds an annual festival (207-647-3699).

▲ SPECIFICALLY FOR SENIORS

Horizons/60 is an active seniors association serving the towns of the Lakes Region. Currently, the program is housed in the Bridgton Community Center, also known as the old Armory. Call 207-647-3116 for more information.

♣ VOLUNTEERING

Friends of the Bridgton Public Library welcomes new members
(207-647-2472), as do Bridgton Hospital (207-647-8841), the Maine
Lakes Chamber of Commerce (207-647-3472), and the Lakes
Environmental Association (207-647-8580; www.mainelakes.org).

*The Bridgton Public Library has a print
collection of more than 23,000 volumes.*

PHOTO BY BILL HAUBERT

Bridgton Public Library
65 Main Street, Bridgton

Hours:
Monday, 10:00 a.m. to 5:00 p.m.
Tuesday and Thursday, 1:00 p.m. to 8:00 p.m.
Wednesday, 1:00 p.m. to 6:00 p.m.
Friday and Saturday, 10:00 a.m. to 2:00 p.m.

Bridgton Public Library first opened in 1895 and moved to its
present location in 1913, with an addition completed in 1994. The
library serves as the community's information center and is home
to far more than just books, even though the print collection numbers more than 23,000 volumes. It also offers more than 700 audio-
visual materials and more than sixty magazines and newspapers.
The Children's Room has more than 7,000 materials in all formats
for a wide range of ages and interests. Bridgton Public Library also
has seven computers, three printers, and a scanner available for
public use. In addition to many other programs, it offers Books-on-
Wheels as well as a full schedule of programs and events for all
ages. Check the Web site at www.bridgton.lib.me.us for more
information.

♣ RECREATION

Golf: Bridgton Highlands Country Club has eighteen holes (207-647-3491); Allen Mountain is a public nine-hole course in nearby Denmark (207-452-2282). **Tennis Courts**: At Bridgton Academy, also at Highland Lake Country Club (207-647-3491). **Parks**: Shorey Park overlooks Highland Lake; several more town spaces are found along Main Street. **Running/Walking/Biking**: Tour maps are available at the Chamber of Commerce. **Fitness Classes**: Bridgton Hospital offers exercise programs (207-647-8841; www.bridgtonhospital.org), as does Horizons/60 (207-647-3116). **Horses/Riding**: Carousel Horse Farm in Casco (207-627-4471; www.carousel-horse-tack-shop.com). **Hunting/Fishing**: Call the Town Office for licenses at 207-647-8786. **Skiing**: Cross-country trails are found at Five Fields Farm (207-647-2425); alpine skiers head to Shawnee Peak (207-647-8444; www.shawneepeak.com) for more than forty trails and glades.

Pleasant Mountain, better known to skiers as Shawnee Peak. PHOTO BY MELISSA ROCK

61

♠ ENTERTAINMENT

Cinemas: Magic Lantern (207-647-5065); Bridgton Drive-In has two screens (207-647-8666). **Theaters**: Deertrees Theatre in Harrison offers ballet, comedy, and drama during the summer (207-583-6747; www.deertreestheatre.org).

♠ NATURE

There are many places to enjoy nature in the Lakes Region. Here are a few: Hold Pond Nature Trail in South Bridgton, the Stevens Brook Trail to Long Lake, Pleasant Mountain, Bald Pate in South Bridgton. The Lakes Environmental Association is dedicated to preserving the natural resources of the Lakes Region (207-647-8580; www.mainelakes.org); Loon Echo Land Trust (207-647-4352) has protected more than 1,000 acres in the area.

♠ SHOPPING

A supermarket and several small grocery stores are located right in Bridgton; larger stores are in North Conway, New Hampshire. The nearest malls are in North Windham, in New Hampshire, and in Portland. A Renys Department Store, plus a number of small specialty stores such as Bridgton Books and Sporthaus, are located downtown.

♠ WHO LIVES HERE

Population: 4,883. **Median Age**: 39.8. **Percentage Age 62 and Older**: 19%. **Percentage with Bachelor's Degree**: 12.9%. **Percentage with Graduate or Professional Degree**: 8.8%. **Median Household Income**: $36,722. **Mean Retirement Income**: $20,184. **Per Capita Income**: $17,352.

♠ ESSENTIAL PHONE NUMBERS AND WEB SITES

Chamber of Commerce: 207-647-3472; www.mainelakeschamber.com. **Town Office**: 207-647-8786. **Voter and Vehicle Registration**:

The Congregational Church on South High Street.
PHOTO BY BILL HAUBERT

Town Clerk's Department (207-647-8786). **Drivers' Licenses:** Motor Vehicle Office in Lewiston (207-753-7750).

⚑ LOCAL NEWS

Newspapers: *Bridgton News* (207-647-2851). **Community Cable Station:** Channel LRTV. **Community Internet Sites:** www.bridgtonnews.com.

⚑ TRANSPORTATION

Closest Airport: Eastern Slope Regional Airport (207-935-2800). **Limo Service:** Timothy's Taxi (888-250-9986). **Train:** North Conway Scenic Railroad is 35 minutes away. **Traffic:** Route 302 runs through the center of town, so traffic can be heavy at certain times of day.

⚑ DISTANCE TO OTHER CITIES

Portland, Me. 38.3 miles
Bangor, Me. 142.2 miles
Boston, Mass. 147.1 miles
New York, N.Y. 346.9 miles
Montreal, Quebec 243.8 miles
Quebec City, Quebec 316.6 miles

↟ JOBS
Bridgton is one of seventeen communities in the Sebago Lakes Region Labor Market. Annual figures for the area in 2001 were: **Civilian Labor Force**: 13,620; **Employed**: 13,100; **Unemployed**: 520; **Unemployment Rate**: 3.8%.

↟ UTILITIES
Electricity: Central Maine Power (800-750-4000). **Water**: 207-647-2881. **Telephone**: Verizon (800-585-4466). **Cable TV**: Adelphia (800-336-9988). **Internet Service Providers**: Adelphia (800-336-9988).

↟ PLACES OF WORSHIP
There are nearly a dozen churches in the area, including Methodist, Congregational, and Catholic congregations. The closest synagogues are located in Portland.

↟ EVENTS AND FESTIVALS
Several seasonal festivals take place in the Lakes Region, including July's Pondicherry Days, a Bridgton event that includes a clambake at the Town Hall, an arts-and-crafts fair held in August, the popular Fryeburg Fair in October, and the annual Mushers Bowl Winter Carnival in February.

↟ RESTAURANTS
Dining choices vary from the timber-beamed Tarry-a-While (207-647-2522) to the moderately priced Venezia (207-647-5333) to the unusual offerings at Tom's Homestead (207-647-5726).

↟ LODGING
Places to stay in the Lakes Region abound, but be sure to check availability first. Tarry-a-While (207-647-2522; www.tarryawhile.com)

is an old summer hotel overlooking Highland Lake. Noble House (207-647-3733; www.noblehousebb.com) is a former senator's manor, nestled among old oaks and pines. Blueberry Hill Resort (207-647-3200) is open all year.

⚑ WHAT THE LOCALS SAY

"My family started vacationing in Bridgton fifty years ago, when I was nine," says Bill Haubert, who moved from Ridgefield, Connecticut, with his wife, Betty, in July 2000. "Betty and I continued summering here with our family, eventually buying our own cabin on one of the many lakes." When Bill retired from IBM several years ago, they decided to build a home and live in Bridgton year-round. "We're on a hill, with views of Pleasant Mountain as well as the White Mountains," says Bill, adding that they enjoy spectacular sunsets nearly every night.

The Hauberts' ties to Bridgton were one of the main reasons they chose to retire in the Lakes Region. "We know this area and the people here well," says Bill. "Over the years, it was easy to get to know the barber, the auto mechanic, the hardware store personnel, the town clerk, and many local people." The Hauberts already belonged to a Bridgton church; since their move, they've found more organizations, such as the Chamber of Commerce, that also welcome their time and expertise. "It's no problem to get connected when you show a genuine interest in being involved," says Bill.

Despite their familiarity with the town, the couple faced a few surprises as year-round residents. "It takes a lot longer to travel to the airport to go see our family in London," says Bill. "It's an hour to get to the mall and a half-hour to get to a major supermarket. And living in a rural area, we're the last on the food chain for technology—things like cable, DSC, and broadband, for instance."

Nevertheless, moving to Bridgton is a lifestyle change the

couple wishes they'd made sooner. "The area offers a four-season vacation living environment," says Bill, "along with a new hospital, an active senior citizens program, friendly people, and lots of volunteer opportunities."

South Portland   *Cumberland County*

At a Glance

Land Area: 13 square miles
Persons per Square Mile: 1,717
Population: 22,324
Median Age: 37.9 years
Neighboring Communities: Cape Elizabeth, Scarborough, Portland, Westbrook

To anyone unfamiliar with the Greater Portland area, it may seem at first glance redundant to include both Portland and South Portland in this book. Aren't they sort of the same place? The answer, in a nutshell, is a resounding "no." While it's true that the two communities have much in common, Portland and its neighbor across the Fore River are two separate and distinct cities; and South Portland, incorporated in 1898, is a destination in its own right.

"South Portland has many unique lifestyle qualities," says realtor Lucille Holt. "It has a friendly atmosphere with many areas to live that are within walking distance of the library, shopping, restaurants, and services." She notes that South Portland, unlike many Maine communities, offers public transportation—a plus for retirees who may not wish to drive. Residents here also have quick and easy access to the Portland Jetport as well as top-notch medical care.

Other amenities that attract retirees include convenient shopping; ample cultural offerings; and a new million-dollar community

The South Portland Community Center, built in 2001, has been a welcome addition to the community. Curtis Walter Stewart Architects designed the building, which is bright and spacious throughout. PHOTOS BY BEN WALTER

center with an indoor swimming pool, aerobic track, and activities for both young and old. Built in 2001, the South Portland Community Center is "definitely the center of this city," says program coordinator Deb Smith. "It has changed the quality of peoples' lives here and impacted our seniors 100%." Residents are also proud of the city's new Liberty Ship Park, which celebrates the time in which "Rosie the Riveter" built hundreds of the so-called "Liberty" cargo ships that many historians credit with helping to win World War II.

Despite its city status, in many ways South Portland operates like a small town. A local horticulturist supplies fresh flowers year-round for the Community Center. A group called Triad organizes volunteers to rake lawns for the elderly. "We have been struck by the widespread civic-mindedness in the greater Portland area," notes newcomer Jeffrey Roberts. "It has been very easy to get connected because the media have kept us informed of numerous opportunities to take part in volunteer activities." Jeffrey and his wife, Bette, have helped the local public radio station, and joined several conservation groups. "We can't imagine a more delightful place to retire than South Portland, Maine," they say. "It is simply a beautiful place to be with all the amenities of gracious living and with people who share an appreciation of life's pleasures in stunning natural surroundings."

▲ WEATHER

Average Temperature (degrees Fahrenheit): January, 21.7; April, 43.7; July, 68.7; October, 47.7. **Average Annual Rainfall:** 44.34 inches. **Average Annual Snowfall:** 71.3 inches

▲ TAXES

Property Tax Rate: $17.06 per $1,000 valuation. **Ratio to Current Market Value:** 85%.

▲ REAL ESTATE

Provided by Lucille Holt, DeWolfe Real Estate (207-761-9400)
Older Housing Stock: $129,000 to $985,000, depending on location. **New Custom Construction:** $275,000 to $400,000. **Waterfront Locations:** $550,000 to $1 million. **Rental Apartments:** $750 to $1,800/month.

▲ RETIREMENT LIVING

Bay Square at Yarmouth (207-846-0044; www.benchmarkquality.com) is a senior living community with both independent and assisted living options. OceanView at Falmouth (207-781-4460) is a few miles northeast of South Portland. Piper Shores (207-883-8700) is located in nearby Scarborough. The Woods at Canco (207-772-4777) is in Portland.

▲ PUBLIC SAFETY

Crimes per 1,000 Population, 2000: 39.89. **Non-emergency Police:** 207-799-5511. **Non-emergency Fire:** 207-799-5511. **Emergency:** 911.

"South Portland is a very safe and friendly community," says Ed Googins, the city's chief of police. "It offers the best qualities of

Maine living to young and old alike. Be it walks along the coast, through Maine's largest shopping mall, or on the Community Center track, there are plenty of opportunities to interact with people and be a part of life here."

⬥ HEALTH CARE

Closest Hospitals: Maine Medical Center (207-871-0111) has 606 acute-care beds, Mercy Hospital (207-879-3000) has 200 acute-care beds, and New England Rehabilitation Center (207-775-4000) has 90 acute-care beds. **Long-Term Care Facilities**: Portland Center for Assisted Living (207-772-2893; www.portlandcenter.com). Eunice Frye Home offers assisted living in a small, newly renovated facility (207-772-6338; www.eunicefrye.com). **Home Health Care**: Community Health Services (207-775-5520).

⬥ CONTINUING EDUCATION

Senior College: Osher Lifelong Learning Institute, University of Southern Maine (800-800-4USM, ext. 8181; www.usm.maine.edu /eap/seniorcollege). **Colleges and Universities**: Husson College (207-775-6512; www.husson.edu); Southern Maine Technical College (207-767-9520; www.smtc.net). **Adult Education Programs**: 207-871-0555.

⬥ LIBRARY

South Portland Public Library (207-767-7660; www.home.maine.rr .com/southportlandlib)

⬥ HISTORICAL SOCIETY

Maine Historical Society (207-774-1822; www.mainehistory.org)

⬥ SPECIFICALLY FOR SENIORS

The Parks and Recreation Department sponsors a senior program

Payson Smith Hall on the campus of the University of Southern Maine is where the Osher Lifelong Learning Institute holds its classes.

PHOTO BY LIBBY BARRETT

offering activities such as computer classes and bridge games at the Community Center as well "lunch and learn" sessions and trips farther afield (207-767-7651).

♠ VOLUNTEERING

Opportunities to volunteer abound at local museums, the library, the hospitals, and conservation groups. Contact the South Portland Community Center (207-767-7651) for specific information.

♠ RECREATION

Golf: South Portland Municipal Golf Course (207-775-0005). Sable Oaks Golf Club is a full-service public golf course (207-775-7160; www.sableoaks.com). **Tennis Courts**: Mill Park Area. **Parks**: Mill Creek Park, Willard Beach, Hinckley Park. **Running/Walking/Biking**: South Portland Community Center (207-767-7651). **Fitness Classes**: South Portland Community Center (207-767-7651). **Hunting/Fishing**: Purchase licenses online at www.informe.org/ifw. **Skiing**: Cross-country skiers use many of the paths through South Portland's parks;

trails are found at Lost Valley Touring Center in Auburn (207-784-1561). Closest downhill area is Lost Valley in Auburn (207-784-1561).

♦ ENTERTAINMENT

The Greater Portland area offers all kinds of things to do. Check out www.visitportland.com for even more ideas. **Cinemas**: Cinemas at Clark Pond. **Museums**: The Center for Maine History (207-774-1822; www.mainehistory.com); Victoria Mansion (207-772-4841; www .victoriamansion.org); Portland Museum of Art (207-775-6148;

South Portland Public Library
482 Broadway, South Portland

Hours:
Monday, Tuesday, and Thursday, 10:00 a.m. to 8:00 p.m.
Wednesday, 1:00 p.m. to 8:00 p.m.
Friday, 10:00 a.m. to 5:00 p.m.
Saturday, 9:00 a.m. to 3:00 p.m.
Closed Saturdays, June through August

South Portland Public Library is located at the intersection of Broadway and Cottage Road, with the parking lot behind the building and the main entrance on Highland Avenue. South Portland Branch Library is on Wescott Road and shares a building with the Municipal Pro-Shop. The main library has a collection of approximately 75,000 volumes, and the Branch has about 16,500 volumes on nearly every subject. Besides books, the libraries offer a fine selection of periodicals for pleasure and research, newspapers, an online magazine database, a growing collection of audio books, videos, music cassettes, and compact discs. Public computers and Internet access are available, as are services for the homebound. Check out both libraries at www.home.maine.rr.com/southportlandlib.com.

---

www.portlandmuseum.org). **Theaters**: Merrill Auditorium (207-874-8200; www.portlandevents.com).

♣ NATURE

The South Portland Land Trust (207-799-4542) has preserved hundreds of acres for conservation. Contact the organization for maps and more information.

♣ SHOPPING

Supermarkets are located by the Maine Mall and in the Mill Creek Area. The mall (207-774-0303), with hundreds of stores, is located in South Portland, as are numerous "big box" stores.

> *South Portland offers wonderful access to Casco Bay for picnicking, boating, and swimming, and yet there are many areas to live that are within walking distance of the library, shopping, restaurants, and services.*
>
> —Lucille Holt,
> DeWolfe Real Estate

♣ WHO LIVES HERE

Population: 23,324. **Median Age**: 37.9. **Percentage Age 62 and Older**: 16.9%. **Percentage with Bachelor's Degree**: 19.3%. **Percentage with Graduate or Professional Degree**: 8.7%. **Median Household Income**: $42,770. **Mean Retirement Income**: $15,052. **Per Capita Income**: $22,781.

♣ ESSENTIAL PHONE NUMBERS AND WEB SITES

Chamber of Commerce: 207-772-2811; www.portlandregion.com. **Convention & Visitors Bureau**: 207-772-5800. **City Hall**: 207-767-3201; www.southportland.org. **Voter Registration**: City Hall (207-767-3201). **Vehicle Registration**: www.informe.org/cgi-bin/bmv/rapid-renewal/rr-1. **Drivers' Licenses**: Motor Vehicle Office (207-822-6400/6417).

♦ LOCAL NEWS

Newspapers: *Portland Press Herald/Maine Sunday Telegram* (207-791-6650; www.portland.com), *Casco Bay Weekly* (207-775-6601; www.cascobayweekly.com), *Portland Phoenix* (207-773-8900; www.portlandphoenix.com). **Community Cable Station**: Channel 4. **Community Internet Sites**: www.southportland.org.

♦ TRANSPORTATION

Bus: Concord Trailways (207-828-1350; www.concordtrailways.com). **Tours**: Duck, walking, and trolley tours abound. Call the Convention & Visitors Bureau (207-772-5800). **Closest Airport**: Portland International Jetport (207-774-7301). **Limo Service**: Airport Limo & Taxi (207-773-3433); Lilley's Limousine (207-741-2121). **Train**: Amtrak, The Downeaster (800-872-7245; www.thedowneaster.com). **Traffic**: The Maine Mall area can be congested at times, but traffic by Mill Creek and on Route 77 is usually pretty light.

♦ DISTANCE TO OTHER CITIES

Portland, Me. 2.3 miles
Bangor, Me. 131.4 miles
Boston, Mass. 110.2 miles
New York, N.Y. 315 miles
Montreal, Quebec 285 miles
Quebec City, Quebec 271.9 miles

♦ JOBS

South Portland is part of Cumberland County. Labor market figures for the area in 2001 were: **Civilian Labor Force**: 145,580; **Employed**: 142,200; **Unemployed**: 3,380; **Unemployment Rate**: 2.3.

♦ UTILITIES

Electricity: Central Maine Power (800-750-4000). **Water**: Portland

Water District (207-761-8310; www.pwd.org). **Telephone:** Verizon (800-585-4466). **Cable TV:** Adelphia (800-336-9988). **Internet Service Providers:** Log On America (207-771-1300; www.loa.com); Prexar LLC (207-283-3627; www.prexar.com).

♦ PLACES OF WORSHIP

There are many churches and temples in the Greater Portland area; call the Maine Council of Churches for more information (207-772-1918). In addition, Portland has three synagogues: Etz Chaim (207-773-2339), Congregation Shaarey Tphiloh (207-773-0693), and Temple Beth El (207-774-2649).

♦ EVENTS AND FESTIVALS

The Greater Portland area is awash in festivals! New Year's Portland kicks off the year, followed by the Old Port Festival in June, the Italian Street Festival in August, the Key Maine Jazz Festival in September, and the Brewer's Festival in November. Check out www.visitportland.com for even more events.

♦ RESTAURANTS

South Portlanders enjoy a wide array of dining choices. Newick's Seafood Restaurant (207-799-3090; www.newicks.com), Barbara's Kitchen and Café (207-767-6313; www.barbaraskitchen.com), and the Saltwater Grille (207-799-5400; www.saltwatergrille.com) are a few to try.

♦ LODGING

Accommodations in South Portland are chain motels and hotels located by the Maine Mall and include: Best Western Merry Manor (207-774-6151; www.bestwestern.com/merrymanorinn), Hampton Inn Hotel (207-773-4400; www.Portlandhamptoninn.com), and Sheraton South Portland (207-775-6161; www.sheraton.com).

⚓ WHAT THE LOCALS SAY

"We had visited South Portland and the surrounding areas during the summers many times and were struck by the natural beauty of this seaside city and its proximity to the beaches, parks, and mountains," say Jeffrey and Bette Roberts, who moved from Massachusetts in 2001. "Though we've always loved the Pleasant Mountain area in the summer and fall, we knew that we could never spend the winter and spring there since there is so little to do that would interest us. Neither of us is a sportsman nor do we enjoy downhill skiing. Having spent our professional lives in the culturally rich region of the five-college area centered in Amherst and Northampton, we were seeking to retire in a bustling city that offered art, music, theater, dance, great restaurants and shopping, and opportunities to meet people socially.

"South Portland and the surrounding area offered us all that and more without the disadvantages of crowds, congestion, traffic, and pollution that plague most major cities. In addition, South Portland's proximity to downtown Portland and the Old Port just across the bridge was very attractive. We are only

The Portland Breakwater Light, or Bug Light, is a well-known South Portland landmark that has recently been restored.

PHOTO BY TED PANAYOTOFF

75

five or ten minutes from everything and yet managed to find a beautiful and affordable home on a private one-acre lot in a quiet neighborhood. Hinckley Park is just a few minutes' walk from here, too."

While the Roberts were familiar with the Greater Portland area, they faced a few surprises as new residents: the state income tax was more than they had expected, and property taxes were higher as well. "Living expenses are always an important consideration for anyone living on a fixed income. Unfortunately, property taxes in South Portland are almost 20% higher than in western Massachusetts. The current fiscal crisis in the state of Maine may cause further cuts in services and additional tax increases."

But Jeffrey and Bette report that the advantages of living here far outweigh the added expenses. "I don't believe we could have found a friendlier city than South Portland. From the caring person who plows our driveway and the man who delivers our mail to the librarians, the municipal employees, store clerks, and people, both young and old, we chance to meet on our daily walks—everyone has been so pleasant and hospitable. We really feel very much at home having lived here just a little over a year."

Portland   *Cumberland County*

At a Glance

Land Area: 19 square miles
Persons per Square Mile: 3,382
Population: 64,249
Median Age: 35.7 years
Neighboring Communities: South Portland, Cape Elizabeth,
     Cumberland, Scarborough, Westbrook, Falmouth

Maine's largest city sits on a hilly peninsula, framed by the Fore River to the west and north, the Presumpscot River to the west and south, and Casco Bay to the east. With a rich 360-year history, the city is a vibrant mix of arts, culture, and charm. Visitors stroll through the historic district called the Old Port, with its cobblestone streets, old-fashioned streetlights, and wide array of shops and fine restaurants. Only minutes away, the city's deepwater port welcomes major international cruise liners, ferries, and shipments of cargo and oil.

There's a small-town feel to Portland, thanks to its livable scale and unique neighborhoods. The Western Promenade features elegant waterfront mansions, while the Eastern Promenade has a spectacular view of island-studded Casco Bay. Deering, the residential section of Portland, is home to much of the city's population. The uptown Arts District features various art galleries, museums, theaters, and a professional symphony orchestra, along with an eclectic mix of stores. Along with the I. M. Pei–designed Portland Museum of Art are two professional sports teams: the Portland Sea Dogs, a Double A baseball team, and the American Hockey League's Portland Pirates.

Not only does Portland feature an active entertainment scene, but its educational opportunities exceed those found in any other part of the state. In addition to the University of Southern Maine, Portland has the Maine College of Art, the University of Maine School of Law, Andover College, and a branch of Bangor-based Husson College. These institutions, along with the city's many arts and athletic organizations, make Portland buzz with activity all year long. Come November, there is no seismic shift of population as occurs in some Maine communities; no "See you next summer" signs taped in storefront windows. Here, truly, is a blending of the pristine beauty of Maine with the advantages of an active and energized city.

For the retiree who thrives on culture, Portland has it all. In addition to plenty of recreational activities, the city boasts superior medical care, top-notch retirement communities, and conveniently close transportation options such as Portland International Jetport and Amtrak's new Downeaster train to Boston. An active senior program sponsored by the Parks and Recreation Department offers activities tailored to older residents, and there are ample opportunities to volunteer at any number of places.

♠ WEATHER
Average Temperature (degrees Fahrenheit): January, 21.7; April, 43.7; July, 68.7; October, 47.7. **Average Annual Rainfall:** 44.34 inches. **Average Annual Snowfall:** 71.3 inches

♠ TAXES
Property Tax Rate: $22.88 per $1,000 valuation. **Ratio to Current Market Value:** 89%.

♠ REAL ESTATE
Provided by Ken Hall of Portland Properties (207-767-4787)
Older Housing Stock: $150,00 to $200,000, depending on location. **New Custom Construction:** $250,000 to $350,00 and up, depending on size and location. **Waterfront Locations:** $350,00 and up. **Rental Apartments:** Furnished, $1,200 to $2,500/month; unfurnished, $500/month.

♠ RETIREMENT LIVING
The Atrium at Cedars (207-775-4111; www.atriumatcedars.com) is an independent living community just minutes from downtown Portland. The Park Danforth (207-797-7710; www.parkdanforth.com) offers 160 apartments and studios. Seventy-Five State Street, in the heart of Portland's West End, offers independent and assisted living (207-772-2675; www.seventyfivestate.com).

Established in 1999, The Atrium is a non-profit, non-sectarian independent living community located just minutes from downtown Portland. Residents enjoy a variety of activities, including golf.

PHOTO BY JON BONJOUR

⚑ PUBLIC SAFETY

Crimes per 1,000 Population, 2000: 45.84. **Non-emergency Police:** 207-874-8300. **Non-emergency Fire:** 207-874-8300. **Emergency:** 911.

Michael Chitwood, Portland's chief of police, says, "As the largest city in the state of Maine, Portland finds itself a uniquely urban environment in a predominantly rural state. As such, our city serves as a major hub for everything from business and entertainment to the provision of social services. Yet despite facing the public safety challenges of urban America, our citizens enjoy a very safe and secure city. This is thanks to the fully capable and professional police force I have the honor to lead, and all of the dedicated public servants in the City of Portland."

⚑ HEALTH CARE

Closest Hospitals: Maine Medical Center (207-871-0111) has 606 acute-care beds, Mercy Hospital (207-879-3000) has 200 acute-care beds, and New England Rehabilitation Center (207-775-4000) has 90 acute-care beds. **Long-Term Care Facilities:** Portland Center for

Assisted Living (207-772-2893; www.portlandcenter.com). Eunice Frye Home offers assisted living in a small, newly renovated facility (207-772-6338; www.eunicefrye.com). **Home Health Care**: Community Health Services (207-775-5520).

♦ CONTINUING EDUCATION

Senior College: Osher Lifelong Learning Institute, University of Southern Maine (800-800-4USM, ext. 8181; www.usm.maine.edu /eap/seniorcollege). **Colleges and Universities**: The state's largest school, the University of Southern Maine (207-780-4141; www.usm .maine.edu), is here, as are several universities and colleges including Andover College (207-774-6126) and Maine College of Art (207-885-3052). **Adult Education Programs**: 207-874-8111; www .portlandadulted.org.

♦ LIBRARY

Portland Public Library (207-871-1700, www.portlandlibrary.com)

♦ HISTORICAL SOCIETY

Maine Historical Society (207-774-1822; www.mainehistory.org)

♦ SPECIFICALLY FOR SENIORS

The Portland Parks and Recreation Department's Senior Program (207-874-8793) offers outings such as dinner followed by an evening at the Portland Museum of Art, plays at the Lyric Theatre and Portland Players, and concerts at Deering Oaks and Fort Allen Park. Luncheons and longer overnight trips to places like New Hampshire and Cape Cod are also offered.

♦ VOLUNTEERING

The Southern Maine Agency on Aging (207-775-6503) is always looking for volunteers for its Retired Senior Volunteer Program, or

RSVP, and is a great clearinghouse for information about volunteer opportunities. Retirees can give their time to a wealth of organizations, from a foster grandparent program to Maine Medical Center.

▲ RECREATION

Golf: Riverside Golf Course has twenty-seven holes plus a full pro shop (207-797-3524). The Nonesuch River Golf Club offers eighteen holes in Scarborough, just minutes from Portland (207-883-0007; www.megolf.com). Tennis Courts: Deering Oaks Park. Parks: Deering Oaks (207-874-8793). Fort Allen Park is on the Eastern Promenade (207-874-8793). Running/Walking/Biking: Portland Trails (207-775-2411; www.trails.org). Fitness Classes: Lifestyle Fitness Center (207-797-5700), Portland Athletic Club (207-781-2671), YWCA (207-874-1130). Hunting/Fishing: Purchase licenses online at

---

Portland Public Library
5 Monument Square, Portland

Hours:
Monday, Wednesday, and Friday, 9:00 a.m. to 6:00 p.m.
Tuesday and Thursday, 12:00 noon to 9:00 p.m.
Saturday, 9:00 a.m. to 5:00 p.m.

Founded in 1867, Portland Public Library has a downtown main library and five neighborhood branch locations. More than 500,000 patrons visit these six locations each year to use one of sixty-five computers; attend free public programs, such as book talks, lectures, educational classes, and book sales; or simply to borrow books. Portland Public Library offers many outreach services, including a Talking Books program. For more information, visit www.portlandlibrary.com.

www.informe.org/ifw. **Skiing**: Cross-country ski trails are found at Smiling Hill Farm in Westbrook (207-775-4815) and at Lost Valley Touring Center in Auburn (207-784-1561); in addition, Nordic enthusiasts use many of the paths in Portland's parks. Closest down-hill ski area is Lost Valley in Auburn (207-784-1561).

♠ ENTERTAINMENT

For a small city, Portland offers a wealth of recreational activities and entertainment options. Check out www.visitportland.com for even more ideas. **Cinemas**: Theaters are located at Canal Plaza and Exchange Street. **Museums**: The Center for Maine History (207-774-1822; www.mainehistory.com); Victoria Mansion (207-772-4841;

The Portland Public Market was opened in 1998. Today, twenty-two vendors sell their wares to customers from Portland and beyond. PHOTO BY CORY MORRISSEY

www.victoriamansion.org); Portland Museum of Art (207-775-6148; www.portlandmuseum.org). **Theaters**: Merrill Auditorium (207-874-8200; www.portlandevents.com).

♠ NATURE

The Fore River Sanctuary is an eighty-five-acre Maine Audubon preserve in Portland (207-781-2330). Baxter Woods is a thirty-acre bird sanctuary and woodland park given to the city by former Governor Percival Baxter.

Portland offers its residents a safe and healthy environment, with low crime, great cultural activities, and Casco Bay and the islands at your doorstep.

—Ken Hall,
Portland Properties

♠ SHOPPING

In addition to the specialty shops of Portland's Downtown District (207-772-6828; www.portlandmaine.com), there is the Portland Public Market on Preble Street (207-228-2000; www.portlandmarket.com) with its fresh Maine foods. The nearest mall is the Maine Mall in nearby South Portland, with more than 100 stores.

♠ WHO LIVES HERE

Population: 64,249. **Median Age**: 35.7. **Percentage Age 62 and Older**: 15.7%. **Percentage with Bachelor's Degree**: 23.4%. **Percentage with Graduate or Professional Degree**: 13%. **Median Household Income**: $35,650. **Mean Retirement Income**: $13,414. **Per Capita Income**: $22,698.

♠ ESSENTIAL PHONE NUMBERS AND WEB SITES

Chamber of Commerce: 207-772-2811; www.portlandregion.com. **Convention & Visitors Bureau**: 207-772-5800. **City Hall**: 207-874-8300; www.ci.portland.me.us. **Voter Registration**: City Hall (207-

874-8677; www.ci.portland.me.us/voter.htm). **Vehicle Registration**: Online at www.informe.org/cgi-bin/bmv/rapid-renewal/rr-1. **Drivers' Licenses**: Motor Vehicle Office (207-822-6400/6417).

♠ LOCAL NEWS

Newspapers: *Portland Press Herald/Maine Sunday Telegram* (207-791-6650; www.portland.com), *Casco Bay Weekly* (207-775-6601; www.cascobayweekly.com), *Portland Phoenix* (207-773-8900; www.portlandphoenix.com). **Community Cable Station**: Channel 4. **Community Internet Sites**: www.ci.portland.me.us.

♠ TRANSPORTATION

Bus: Concord Trailways (207-828-1350; www.concordtrailways.com). **Tours**: Duck, walking, and trolley tours abound. Call the Convention & Visitors Bureau (207-772-5800). **Closest Airport**: Portland International Jetport (207-774-7301). **Limo Service**: Airport Limo & Taxi (207-773-3433), Lilley's Limousine (207-741-2121). **Train**: Amtrak, The Downeaster (800-872-7245; www.TheDowneaster.com). **Traffic**: Busy at rush hour.

♠ DISTANCE TO OTHER CITIES

Bangor, Me. 129 miles
Boston, Mass. 112.5
New York, N.Y. 317.3 miles
Montreal, Quebec 282.7
Quebec City, Quebec 269.6 miles

♠ JOBS

Portland is part of Cumberland County. Labor market figures for the area in 2001 were: **Civilian Labor Force**: 145,580; **Employed**: 142,200; **Unemployed**: 3,380; **Unemployment Rate**: 2.3%.

♠ UTILITIES

Electricity: Central Maine Power (800-750-4000). **Water**: Portland Water District (207-761-8310; www.pwd.org). **Telephone**: Verizon (800-585-4466). **Cable TV**: Adelphia (800-336-9988). **Internet Service Providers**: Log On America (207-771-1300; www.loa.com), Prexar LLC (207-283-3627; www.prexar.com).

♠ PLACES OF WORSHIP

There are many churches and temples in the Greater Portland area; call the Maine Council of Churches for more information (207-772-1918). In addition, Portland has three synagogues: Etz Chaim (207-773-2339), Congregation Shaarey Tphiloh (207-773-0693), and Temple Beth El (207-774-2649).

♠ EVENTS AND FESTIVALS

The Greater Portland area is awash in festivals! New Year's Portland kicks off the year, followed by the Old Port Festival in June, the Italian Street Festival in August, the Key Maine Jazz Festival in September, and the Brewer's Festival in November. Check out www .visitportland.com for even more events.

♠ RESTAURANTS

Not long ago, Portland had more restaurants per capita than any other U.S. city except San Francisco. It still has loads of eateries, everything from The Flatbread Company (207-772-8777) to Café Uffal (207-775-3380) to the famous DiMillo's Floating Restaurant (207-772-2216).

♠ LODGING

All types of lodging and all price ranges are represented in Greater Portland. The Inn at St. John (207-773-6481; www.innatstjohn.com)

offers historical charm, the Eastland Park Hotel (207-775-5411; www.eastlandparkhotel.com) is a downtown landmark with a rooftop lounge, and the West End Inn (207-772-1377; www.westendbb.com) looks out over the Western Promenade.

♣ WHAT THE LOCALS SAY

Rhea Freedman moved to Portland from Florida in April 2001 to be nearer to her two daughters and their families. Needless to say, one of her biggest concerns coming from the Sunshine State was the severity of winter in coastal Maine. "I thought the weather might be a real downside to living here," she admits. "But coming originally from New York, I haven't found it much of a shock."

Rhea had visited Portland on many occasions, and though she felt well-informed about the area, she was initially concerned about housing and medical resources. "I have an apartment at the Park Danforth, and I've found that Portland is very good to its seniors. Most people and services are caring and genuinely interested in my welfare."

Local activities offered by both the city and the Park Danforth have made for an active retirement for Rhea. "It took me a little while to figure out what I wanted to do, but now I'm fairly busy," she says. She takes advantage of trips and luncheons offered through Portland Parks and Recreation's Senior Program and is an active volunteer at the YMCA.

While she enjoys the amenities of the Port City, she credits her family with having made her transition to Maine so smooth. "It is important to have a family who cares about your well-being in any location," she believes. "In my opinion, this is the most important factor in the senior years."

♣♣♣

Brunswick
Cumberland County

At a Glance

Land Area: 46.78 square miles
Persons per Square Mile: 452
Population: 21,172
Median Age: 35.5 years
Neighboring Communities: Bath, Topsham, Freeport, Harpswell

Originally settled in 1628 along the falls of the Androscoggin River, Brunswick is an eclectic mix: part college town, part Navy base, and part traditional New England village. Centers for both the University of Maine and Southern New Hampshire University are located here, offering a wide range of associate, bachelor's, and even a few master's degrees. A branch of Embry-Riddle Aeronautical University instructs would-be pilots in aviation skills. Finally, some 1,600 students attend venerable Bowdoin College, whose famous graduates include Henry Wadsworth Longfellow and Civil War general Joshua Chamberlain. Founded in 1794, Bowdoin's long tenure as a prestigious liberal arts institution gives Brunswick the distinction of being Maine's oldest college community.

Equally impressive is the Naval Air Station (NAS), located across town. The last active-duty Department of Defense airfield remaining in the Northeast, NAS Brunswick is home to five active-duty and two reserve squadrons. About a fifth of the station's activities support the AEGIS Destroyer shipbuilding program at nearby Bath Iron Works. The air station employs 4,863 military and civilian personnel, including 713 officers, 3,493 enlisted personnel, and 657 civilians, making it Maine's second largest employer. "The Naval Air Station is an active and integral part of the local community," says real estate broker Dave Gleason. In addition to its social and cultural contributions, it pumps more than $187 million into the local economy, including $115 million in salaries, $38 million in contracts and materiel purchases, and $34 million in medical supply purchases.

Despite its size and activity level, Brunswick retains its village character. There's a thriving downtown, bisected by the state's widest main thoroughfare, Maine Street. Here, stores, eateries, offices, and service establishments contribute the kind of hustle-bustle and friendly banter that make for a lively sense of community. Another commercial area, Cook's Corner, features large chain stores, fast-food restaurants, and supermarkets. But Brunswick's not all business: there are literally miles and miles of quiet places to walk, bike, or paddle. In addition to the grassy, tree-lined Town Mall, there's the popular Androscoggin River Bike Bath, a two-plus-mile paved pathway frequented by bikers, joggers, and those just out for a stroll.

In many ways, Brunswick seems to have it all. The cities of Portland and Augusta are only thirty miles away, and the Harpswells—two peninsulas peppered with quaint fishing villages—are even closer. A wide range of cultural opportunities awaits the retiree who enjoys the performing arts: Bowdoin alone sponsors close to 300 concerts, lectures, and performances a year, most of which are open to the public at little or no cost. The pull of history is evident in several National Historic Districts, and a legacy of fine shipbuilding lies just up the coast in Bath. Lastly, thanks to the colleges and the Naval Air Station, Brunswick boasts an ethnic and racial diversity not found in many parts of Maine.

It's an invigorating mix, recognized by the national media a few years back when *Money* magazine named Brunswick its top place to retire in New England. Those who live here note that education, arts, and community have always been Brunswick trademarks. After all, this is where Longfellow studied and where Harriet Beecher Stowe wrote *Uncle Tom's Cabin*. Chief of Police Jerry Hinton sums it up this way: "Brunswick is a great community with many amenities, including exceptional schools and super libraries, with both public and college resources. In addition, we have a wonderful relationship with our military and marine life heritage."

⚑ WEATHER

Average Temperature (degrees Fahrenheit): January, 20.6; April, 43.6; July, 68.9; October, 48. **Average Annual Rainfall:** 45.23 inches. **Average Annual Snowfall:** 75.9 inches.

⚑ TAXES

Property Tax Rate: $21 per $1,000 valuation. **Ratio to Current Market Value:** 85%.

⚑ REAL ESTATE

Provided by Dave Gleason, Coldwell Banker Residential Brokerage (207-725-8522)
Older Housing Stock: $150,000 to $300,000. **New Custom Construction:** $225,000 to $425,000. **Waterfront Locations:** $300,000 to $600,000. **Rental Apartments:** $550 to $700/month.

> *Why do people retire in Brunswick? I think they're looking for an invigorating community and a little peace of mind.*
>
> —Dave Gleason,
> Coldwell Banker
> Residential Brokerage

⚑ RETIREMENT LIVING

Thornton Oaks (800-729-8033; www.thorntonoaks.com) is located on twenty-nine acres adjacent to Mid Coast Hospital, only blocks from Bowdoin College and Maine Street, and offers residents independent apartments, cottages, and assisted-living units. The Highlands, with 285 residents, is located in nearby Topsham (888-760-1042; www.highlandsrc.com).

Retirement living at Thornton Oaks is just blocks from Bowdoin College and Maine Street. PHOTO COURTESY OF THORNTON OAKS

♠ PUBLIC SAFETY

Crimes per 1,000 Population, 2000: 28.12. **Non-emergency Police**: 207-725-551; www.brunswickpd.org. **Non-emergency Fire**: 207-725-5541. **Emergency**: 911.

"As the largest 'town' in Maine, we are also one of the safest relative to our local and service populations," says Police Chief Jerry Hinton. "Our highly educated and skilled men and women in public service strive to make this a great place to live."

♠ HEALTH CARE

Closest Hospitals: Mid Coast Hospital (207-729-0181; www.midcoasthealth.com) offers a complete range of inpatient and outpatient services, including surgery, diagnostic testing, and a twenty-four-hour emergency care center. Parkview Hospital is a 55-bed,

acute-care community hospital (207-373-2000; www.parkviewhospital
.org). **Home Health Care**: Community Health and Nursing Services
(207-729-6782). **Long-Term Care Facilities**: Skolfield House (207-
725-5801), Dionne Commons (207-729-4379), Bodwell House (207-
373-3600), The Stevens Home (207-725-5701).

⚑ CONTINUING EDUCATION

Senior College: Midcoast Senior College is located at University
College of Bath/Brunswick (207-725-8620). **Colleges and Universities**:
University of Maine Bath–Brunswick Center (207-725-8620; www
.maine.edu), Southern New Hampshire University at Brunswick Cen-
ter (207-725-6486, www.snhu.edu). Seniors can audit many courses
at Bowdoin College (207-725-3375, www.bowdoin.edu). **Adult
Education Programs**: Brunswick High School (207-798-5500).
Elderhostel: Summer program at Bowdoin College (207-725-3375).

⚑ LIBRARY

Curtis Memorial Library (207-725-5242; www.curtislibrary.com)

⚑ HISTORICAL SOCIETY

The Pejepscot Historical Society (207-729-6606) is very active and
owns three museums in town.

⚑ SPECIFICALLY FOR SENIORS

The 55 Plus Center (207-729-0757; www.55pluscenter.org) offers
advocacy along with organized social, recreational, and educational
programs (such as classes in tai chi), an informal theater group, and
lunches out.

⚑ VOLUNTEERING

Some of the many local nonprofits that welcome volunteers are: the
American Cancer Society (207-729-3339), Big Brothers/Big Sisters

(207-729-7736), Literacy Volunteers (207-725-1612), and Volunteers of America (207-373-1140). There are also many clubs, including the Association of Bowdoin Friends (207-725-3375) and the Kennebec Art Club in Bath (207-443-4695).

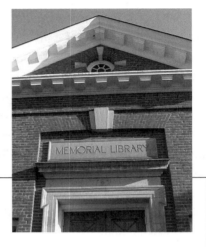

Curtis Memorial Library is on Pleasant Street in Brunswick.

PHOTO BY MICHAEL HEATH,
COURTESY OF CURTIS MEMORIAL LIBRARY

Curtis Memorial Library
23 Pleasant Street, Brunswick

Hours:
Monday through Thursday, 9:30 a.m. to 8:00 p.m.
Friday, 9:30 a.m. to 6:00 p.m.
Saturday, 9:30 a.m. to 5:00 p.m. (in summer until 1:00 p.m.)
Sunday, 1:00 p.m. to 5:00 p.m. (closed in summer)

The original library building was completed in 1904 and dedicated to John Curtis, a celebrated ship's captain who sailed from the Brunswick area to ports around the world in the second half of the nineteenth century. In October 1999, an expanded and renovated $6.2 million facility was completed and features more than 300 user spaces and a community meeting room. Curtis Library boasts many services, including a high-speed network of more than 100 terminals for public and staff use, interlibrary loan, and community programs. The library aims to add 15,000 new items yearly to a collection that now exceeds 115,000 items. For more information, see www.curtislibrary.com.

♣ RECREATION

Golf: Brunswick Golf Club (207-725-8224) is a public course offering eighteen challenging holes; Long Shot Golf Range (207-725-6377) is the place to practice your drive. **Tennis Courts**: By the old high school on McKean Street; also at Maine Pines (207-729-8433, www.mainepines.com). **Parks**: Bay Bridge Landing Interpretive Trail (.3-mile loop), Town Commons. **Running/Walking/Biking**: Androscoggin River Bike Path (2.64 miles), Town Commons (Pitch Pine Barren Loop). Cox Pinnacle, the highest point of land in Brunswick, boasts a view of the White Mountains. **Fitness Classes**: Casco Bay YMCA (207-865-9600, www.cascobayymca.org), Maine Pines (207-729-8433, www.mainepines.com), Cellar of Fitness (207-721-0007). **Horses/Riding**: Sable Oaks Equestrian Center (207-443-4006).

Just one of the challenging holes at the Brunswick Golf Club. PHOTO BY CHRIS DOYLE

Hunting: Town Clerk's Department (207-725-6658, www.curtislibrary .com/townclerk). **Fishing**: Town Clerk's Department (207-725-6658, www.curtislibrary.com/townclerk) issues licenses; sportfishing charters are also available. **Skiing**: The Town Commons offers four seasons of enjoyment, with trails accessible for cross-country skiing and snowshoeing in winter. Trails for cross-country skiing are also found on Route 123. The closest downhill ski area is Lost Valley in Auburn (207-784-1561), with fifteen trails and three lifts.

⚜ ENTERTAINMENT
Cinemas: Eveningstar Cinema; Hoyt's Brunswick Cinema Ten. **Museums**: Bowdoin College Museum of Art (207-725-3275); Peary-MacMillan Arctic Museum (207-725-3416); Joshua Chamberlain Museum, Pejepscot Museum, Skolfield-Whittier House (all 729-6606). **Theaters**: Maine State Music Theatre (207-725-8769); The Theatre Project (207-729-8584).

FINDING THE CENTER
Brunswick and the surrounding towns of Topsham, Phippsburg, Georgetown, Harpswell, Wiscasset, and Freeport, as well as the neighboring city of Bath, constitute a geographic region often referred to as the Midcoast. Confusion arises because the Camden–Rockport–Rockland area to the north lays claim to the same designation. Who's really in the middle? Judy Hayes, a cartographer with the DeLorme mapmaking company in Yarmouth, says, "As the crow flies from Kittery to Lubec, Camden–Rockland is the approximate midpoint. Brunswick and Bath are often considered the gateways to the midcoast region, which extends beyond the Camden–Rockland midpoint to the eastern rim of Penobscot Bay."

⬆ NATURE

The Bowdoin Pines Trail lies in a thirty-three-acre site adjacent to the corner of Federal Street and the Bath Road. Captain Alfred Skolfield Nature Preserve is an eleven-acre preserve owned and maintained by the Brunswick–Topsham Land Trust. It lies adjacent to Merriconeag Road between Middle Bay Cove and Harpswell Cove.

⬆ SHOPPING

Supermarkets are located in the downtown area and at Cook's Corner. Large stores such as Sears and Wal-Mart are also found at Cook's Corner. Retirees who are veterans can shop at the Naval Air Station commissary. The nearest mall is the Maine Mall in South Portland, about thirty miles away. Numerous small specialty stores are located downtown along Maine Street, offering everything one would expect to find in a college town.

⬆ WHO LIVES HERE

Population: 21,172. **Median Age**: 35.5. **Percentage Age 62 and Older**: 17.8%. **Percentage with Bachelor's Degree**: 20.1%. **Percentage with Graduate or Professional Degree**: 14.9%. **Median Household Income**: $40,402. **Mean Retirement Income**: $17,777. **Per Capita Income**: $20,322.

⬆ ESSENTIAL PHONE NUMBERS AND WEB SITES

Chamber of Commerce: 207-725-8797; www.midcoastmaine.com. **Town Office**: 207-725-6653, www.brunswickme.org. **Voter and Vehicle Registration**: Town Finance Department (207-725-6652). **Drivers' Licenses**: Motor Vehicle Office (207-725-6520).

⬆ LOCAL NEWS

Newspapers: *The Times Record* (207-729-3311), *Coastal Journal* (207-443-6241). **Community Cable Station**: Channel 7.

⬆ TRANSPORTATION

Bus: Coastal Trans Bus Service (207-443-6207). Vermont Transit/ Greyhound Bus stops in Brunswick, as does Concord Trailways. **Taxi**: Bath Taxi (207-443-4009). **Closest Airport**: Portland International Jetport (forty minutes away). **Train**: Amtrak to Boston's South Station or Route 128 from Portland; Brunswick will be on the line by 2004. **Traffic**: Usually light; moderate in season.

⬆ DISTANCE TO OTHER CITIES

Portland, Me. 26 miles

Bangor, Me. 107 miles

Boston, Mass. 137 miles

New York, N.Y. 342 miles

Montreal, Quebec 257 miles

Quebec City, Quebec 246 miles

⬆ JOBS

Brunswick is one of twenty-one communities in the Bath/Brunswick Labor Market. Annual figures for the area in 2001 were: **Civilian Labor Force**: 35,140; **Employed**: 34,060; **Unemployed**: 1,080; **Unemployment Rate**: 3.1%.

⬆ UTILITIES

Electricity: Central Maine Power (207-721-8020). **Water**: Brunswick– Topsham Water District (207-729-9956). **Sewer**: Brunswick Sewer (207-729-0148). **Telephone**: Verizon (800-585-4466). **Cable TV**: Susquehanna Communications (207-729-6663). **Internet Service Providers**: EnvisioNet (207-373-3200).

⬆ PLACES OF WORSHIP

Protestant, Catholic, and interdenominational churches abound.

The closest synagogue, Beth Israel Congregation (207-443-3062) is located in nearby Bath.

⚑ EVENTS AND FESTIVALS

In addition to a summer music festival held at Bowdoin in July and August, Thomas Point Beach, located on tidal water in Brunswick, hosts three annual festivals. The four-day Maine Festival features performing arts and craftspeople; the Maine Highland Games presents bagpipe bands, dancing, and folk singing; and the Labor Day Bluegrass Festival features—you guessed it—bluegrass music.

⚑ RESTAURANTS

Dining choices vary from neighborhood delicatessens to Indian cuisine to traditional seafood. Here are just a few of Brunswick's many eateries: Joshua's Restaurant & Tavern (207-725-7981), Harriet Beecher Stowe House (207-729-7869), MacMillan & Co. (207-729-9662), Richard's (207-729-9673).

⚑ LODGING

There are dozens of hotels, motels, inns, and bed-and-breakfast establishments. A small sampling follows (be sure to book ahead at these or any other lodging places, especially during the summer or holidays): Comfort Inn (207-729-1129), Brunswick Bed & Breakfast (207-729-4914, www.brunswickbnb.com), Middle Bay Farm B&B (207-373-1375).

⚑ WHAT THE LOCALS SAY

Marjorie and Kenneth Smith had summered in Maine for forty years before deciding to retire here in 2001. "Our daughter and son-in-law, plus two grandsons, live in Portland," says Kenneth. "We knew we wanted to be near them." After selling a home in Newark, Delaware, the couple moved into a sunny private house in the Brunswick retirement community of Thornton Oaks. "We visited several places," says Kenneth. "But after our second visit to Thornton Oaks, we decided that it was our first choice. We have been surprised to find how pleased and happy we are to be residents of this community."

The Smiths cite many advantages to living in Brunswick, among them the cultural offerings at Bowdoin College and the proximity to Portland and its cultural and recreational opportunities. They enjoy Brunswick's beautiful surroundings, as well as the sense of safety and security they experience, both in the town and at Thornton Oaks. A homeowners cooperative affiliated with, but not owned by, nearby Mid Coast Hospital, Thornton Oaks offers residents a lively social calendar as well as privileges such as use of the dining room. "The services provided by the staff here are outstanding," notes Kenneth. "We heartily recommend this place to anyone considering a fine retirement community."

Kenneth and Marjorie suggest making several visits to Maine before finalizing any retirement plans. "Get to know the area during several seasons of the year," says Kenneth. "Know why you want to come so that you'll make a good choice." Before moving, the Smiths made sure their retirement funds were adequate for their new lifestyle and waited until some serious health problems were resolved. "It was tough to shrink down our possessions from a very large house to a very small one," he says. "But we both feel that moving here was a good decision. We love being close to our Portland family, as well as our summer home, and we've made many new friends."

▲▲▲

Western Mountains

Two counties—Oxford and Franklin—make up the western mountain region, although both of the towns profiled in this book are located within Franklin County's borders. Tall peaks, pristine lakes, and recreation magnets such as the ski areas of Sunday River, Saddleback, and Sugarloaf/USA attract visitors to this part of the state, and some find they do not want to leave.

Thanks to skiing, hiking, fishing, and leaf peeping, tourism is one of the main industries in this neck of the woods, but equally important is the manufacture of pulp and paper in towns such as Jay and Rumford. Commercially, Bethel is the center of activity in Oxford County, while Farmington serves both as Franklin County's shire town and economic hub.

Population-wise, Franklin is one of Maine's smaller counties: there are no cities in Franklin; however, Farmington, a town with a friendly attitude and a University of Maine campus, boasts a surprising amount of cultural activity. This college town is one of the western mountain communities profiled in this book; the other, the quietly impressive town of Rangeley, home of the famed Rangeley Lakes and surrounding forests.

Retirement villages are practically nonexistent here, and both Farmington and Rangeley appeal to people desiring an active, outdoor lifestyle. With mountains, streams, and more than 100 lakes and ponds, this part of Maine is as beautiful and unspoiled as it gets. Other towns in Franklin County include Wilton, home of the only fiddlehead (an edible fern) canning factory in the country, and Weld, a small community of 500 or so and site of eight-mile-long Webb Lake.

Farmington

Franklin County

At a Glance

Land Area: 55 square miles
Persons per Square Mile: 135
Population: 7,410
Median Age: 31.6 years
Neighboring Communities: Temple, Wilton, Chesterville, New Sharon

Click on this town's Web site, and here's what you find: "Farmington extends a warm invitation to retirees to experience life in our beautiful, healthy, culturally and educationally active community." It's tough to get any more welcoming than that, and hard to name a place with the same mix of rural charm and cultural savvy as this western mountains college town.

The shire town of Franklin County, Farmington was settled just after the Revolutionary War and incorporated in 1794. Encompassing fifty-four gently rolling square miles, including the neighborhoods of Farmington Falls and West Farmington, Farmington serves as the cultural, educational, social, and shopping hub of the area. The town has many amenities, including its own radio station (99.3 WKTJ-FM), twice-weekly newspaper, restaurants ranging from popular diners to upscale dining facilities, a friendly ski slope, and several museums.

Part of the appeal here is due to the University of Maine at Farmington (UMF). Established in 1864 as Maine's first public institution of higher education, UMF has earned a national reputation for excellence and value, garnering accolades from *U.S. News & World Report* and others. For residents, UMF not only provides educational opportunities, but cultural offerings as well. Public readings by Pulitzer Prize–winning poets, performances by nationally and internationally known dance troupes, musicians, and comedians, and art

Farmington's downtown offers a lively mix of stores, restaurants, and businesses.

PHOTO BY SABRA STIRLING, COURTESY OF THE FARMINGTON CHAMBER OF COMMERCE

gallery exhibits by renowned artists are all part of the town's cultural landscape, thanks, in large part, to the university.

UMF and Farmington collaborate in many ways. An on-campus Health and Fitness Center is used by both the university community and townspeople. The town and campus also cooperated in a drive that raised more than $1 million to expand both the university and community libraries.

Other perks that make retiring here rewarding include an expanding hospital, a lively downtown, and several buildings listed in the National Register of Historic Sites. As Sandy Gregor, community center coordinator for Seniors Plus in Wilton, puts it, "Everybody thinks about the coast, but this area is one of the best-kept secrets in Maine."

⚑ WEATHER

Average Temperature (degrees Fahrenheit): January, 14.4; April, 40.2; July, 65.9; October, 44.9. **Average Annual Rainfall:** 45.54 inches. **Average Annual Snowfall:** 93.2 inches.

⚑ TAXES

Property Tax Rate: $17.85 per $1,000 valuation. **Ratio to Current Market Value:** 100%.

♠ REAL ESTATE

Provided by Juanita Bean Smith, Bean & Smith Real Estate (207-778-4374)
Older Housing Stock: $90,000 to $250,000, depending on location.
New Custom Construction: $100/square foot and up, depending on size and location. **Waterfront Locations**: $200,000 and up. **Riverfront Lots**: $35,000. **Rental Apartments**: $650/month.

♠ RETIREMENT LIVING

Orchard Park Congregate Apartments (207-778-4416) are one-bedroom apartments with 24-hour support services on site.

♠ PUBLIC SAFETY

Crimes per 1,000 Population, 2000: 32.05. **Non-emergency Police**: 207-778-6311. **Non-emergency Fire**: 207-778-3235. **Emergency**: 911.

Richard E. Caton, Farmington's chief of police, says that his community has a cohesiveness that makes working for the town a pleasure. "It's a relatively small community, even though we're the service area and seat of the county, but we have wonderful citizens involved in town affairs. We have our ups and downs with minor things, but I'd say Farmington is a safe, rural, Maine community, clearly safer than many parts of the country." He gives newcomers this advice: "Go the speed limit through town. We're pretty strict about it."

♠ HEALTH CARE

Closest Hospitals: Franklin Memorial Hospital (207-778-6031, www .fchn.org), in Farmington, is a 70-bed, acute-care community general hospital that offers a wide range of medical, surgical, obstetric, pediatric, and state-of-the-art technological services. The hospital has begun a $12.5 million expansion that will include an ambulatory surgical center, family-centered birthing and pediatric units, a new health education center, a helipad, and renovations to the surgical suite and

outpatient medical clinics. **Long-Term Care Facilities**: Edgewood
Rehabilitation and Living Center (207-778-3386), Orchard Park
Rehabilitation and Living Center (207-778-4416), Sandy River Center
for Health Care and Rehabilitation (207-778-6591). **Hospice**: Androscoggin Home Care and Hospice (207-645-5334).

♣ CONTINUING EDUCATION

Senior College: Gold Leaf Institute at the University of Maine at
Farmington (207-778-7063). **Colleges and Universities**: University
of Maine at Farmington (207-778-7000; www.umf.maine.edu).
Adult Education Programs: Franklin County Adult Learning Center
(207-778-3460).

♣ LIBRARY

Farmington Public Library (207-778-4312; www.farmington.lib.me.us).

*The University of Maine at Farmington was the state's first public institution of
higher learning.* PHOTO BY TOM DONAGHUE

♠ HISTORICAL SOCIETY
Farmington Historical Society (207-778-3106).

♠ SPECIFICALLY FOR SENIORS
SeniorsPlus coordinates the Senior Center in Wilton (207-645-3315), open to residents of Franklin County. The center offers community dining sites; regular activities and trips; and classes in fitness, nutrition, and other topics of interest.

♠ VOLUNTEERING
Meals on Wheels (207-645-3315), Franklin Memorial Hospital (207-778-6031), and School Administrative District 9 (207-778-3460) all welcome volunteer involvement.

Farmington Public Library
117 Academy Street, Farmington

Hours:
Tuesday and Wednesday, 10:00 a.m. to 8:00 p.m.
Thursday and Friday, 10:00 a.m. to 6:00 p.m.
Saturday, 10:00 a.m. to 2:00 p.m. (10:00 a.m. to 12:00 noon in July and August)

In 1890, the current Farmington Public Library Association was incorporated and continues to serve the community and the region. The library's collection of 30,000 items focuses on popular reading for adults as well as large-print books, magazines, and audio books. The library also has a notable collection of Maine authors, local and town history, and a genealogy reference library. Services include photocopying, reference and genealogy assistance, interlibrary loan, public computers, and adult reading/discussion programs. See www.farmington.lib.me.us.

↟ RECREATION

Golf: Wilson Lake Country Club (207-645-2016) in Wilton is a nine-hole public course. **Tennis Courts**: Hippach Field has outdoor courts; the UMF Health and Fitness Center offers indoor tennis by reservation (207-778-7495). **Parks**: Hippach Field, Meetinghouse Park (by the Superior Court Building). West Farmington has Walton Mill Park. **Running/Walking/Biking**: Trails are found by Franklin Memorial Hospital. **Fitness Classes**: Seniors pay a small fee to use the UMF Health and Fitness Center, which includes an indoor pool, track, weight room, and classes. **Horses/Riding**: Knowlton Corner Farm (207-778-6520; www.knowltoncorner.com). **Hunting/Fishing**: Call the Town Office for licenses at 207-778-6538. **Skiing**: Cross-country trails and downhill skiing are in town at Titcomb Mountain (207-778-9031; www.titcombmountain.com). Troll Valley (207-778-3656) also offers cross-country skiing.

> *Farmington is just large enough to offer a broad selection of cultural and recreational activities, a well-staffed, up-to-date hospital and related medical services, plus enough shops to satisfy your needs and some of your extravagances. It's just small enough so that it's easy to meet people, make friends, and participate in the community.*
>
> —Juanita Bean Smith,
> Bean & Smith Real Estate

↟ ENTERTAINMENT

Cinemas: Narrow Gauge Cinemas (207-778-4877). **Museums**: Red School House Museum (207-778-4215), Stanley Museum (207-265-2729). The Nordica Memorial Association (207-778-2856) celebrates the achievements of twentieth-century opera star Lillian Nordica. **Theaters**: Lakewood Theater, the nation's oldest summer theater (207-474-7176; www.lakewoodtheater.org). **Music**: Arts Institute of

Western Maine (207-778-7136; www.artsinstitute.org) has a calendar of area performances.

↟ NATURE

A small nature area is on the grounds of UMF. Nearby Mount Blue State Park in Weld offers hiking, camping, and recreation on beautiful Webb Lake.

↟ SHOPPING

Supermarkets are located on the Wilton Road (Routes 2 and 4) and in the Mount Blue Shopping Area. Small grocery stores are found on Main Street. A small mall is in Auburn; larger malls in Portland and Bangor are about one-and-a-half hours distant. Downtown Farmington has all kinds of small specialty stores, such as Devaney Doak & Garrett Booksellers (207-778-3454), Bouffard's Furniture (207-778-2045), and Howard's Rexall Drugstore on Main Street (800-371-2695, www.howardsrexall.com), where you can not only fill a prescription but also place a JC Penney order, ship UPS, and rent a video!

↟ WHO LIVES HERE

Population: 7,410. Median Age: 31.6. Percentage Age 62 and Older: 17.8%. Percentage with Bachelor's Degree: 17.4%. Percentage with Graduate or Professional Degree: 9.1%. Median Household Income: $28,614. Mean Retirement Income: $11,351. Per Capita Income: $13,982.

↟ ESSENTIAL PHONE NUMBERS AND WEB SITES

Chamber of Commerce: 207-778-4215; www.Farmingtonchamber.org. Town Office: 207-778-6538, www.farmington-maine.org. Voter and Vehicle Registration: Town Clerk's Department (207-778-6538). Drivers' Licenses: A mobile unit of the Motor Vehicle Office comes to the Elks Lodge on the first and last Wednesday of each month.

↥ LOCAL NEWS

Newspapers: *Franklin Journal* (207-778-2075), *Lewiston Sun-Journal* (207-778-6772). **Community Cable Station**: Channel 11. **Community Internet Sites**: www.farmington-maine.org, www.farmingtonchamber.org.

↥ TRANSPORTATION

Bus: Buses for the elderly/disabled are provided by Western Maine Transportation Services (207-364-2135). **Tours**: UMF gives campus tours. **Closest Airport**: Portland or Bangor. **Limo Service**: Western Maine Transportation Services (207-364-2135). **Traffic**: Very manageable. As Juanita Bean Smith says, "A Main Street parking spot is as easily found in August as in February!"

↥ UTILITIES

Electricity: Central Maine Power (800-750-4000). **Water**: Farmington Water Department (207-778-4777). **Telephone**: Verizon (800-585-4466). **Cable TV**: Adelphia (800-336-9988). **Internet Service Providers**: Route2.com (207-778-4977; www.route2.com).

↥ DISTANCE TO OTHER CITIES

Portland, Me. 91 miles
Bangor, Me. 79.8
Boston, Mass. 186.4 miles
New York, N.Y. 391.2 miles
Montreal, Quebec 221.8 miles
Quebec City, Quebec 196.4 miles

↥ JOBS

Farmington is one of twenty-four communities and several unorganized territories in the Farmington Labor Market. Annual figures for the area in 2001 were: **Civilian Labor Force**: 17,080; **Employed**: 15,950; **Unemployed**: 1,130; **Unemployment Rate**: 6.6%.

♠ PLACES OF WORSHIP

More than a dozen churches call Farmington home, including the
Henderson Memorial Baptist Church and the Religious Society of
Friends. The closest synagogue is Beth Israel, located in Waterville
(207-872-7551).

♠ EVENTS AND FESTIVALS

The Children's Festival is held each February, and everyone in the
area turns out for the Franklin County Fair in September. The first
Saturday in December celebrates Chester Greenwood, the famous
native son who, at the age of 15, invented the earmuff to keep
himself warm while ice-skating.

♠ RESTAURANTS

College towns offer eclectic eating places, and Farmington is no
exception. There are the Granary Brew Pub (207-779-0710), Java
Joe's Corner Café (207-779-1000), the venerable Farmington Diner
(207-778-4151), and more.

♠ LODGING

Stay in quaint old homes such as Blackberry Farm Bed & Breakfast
(207-778-2035) and County Seat Inn B & B (207-778-3901) as well
as convenient motels such as Twin Pond Motel (800-245-4977) and
Farmington Motel (207-778-2805).

♠ WHAT THE LOCALS SAY

"I moved to Farmington in 1944 at eleven years of age," says Charles
Murray, a retired shoe manufacturing manager. "But in 1980, business
took us away to other parts of the country: Wisconsin, Tennessee,
and New York." Thirteen years later, Charles and his family moved
back to Farmington. "We'd lived here before and knew its many

advantages," he says. "Yet we were concerned that the town would not offer us the cultural activities we'd enjoyed in other locations."

The Murrays returned to find only pleasant surprises in their old hometown. "During our years of absence, the town had changed due to the growth of the university and hospital, and the results are wonderful. Farmington offers a retiree a small-town tempo and way of life, combined with the cultural advantages of a highly ranked university—not only art, music, and lectures, but facilities such as an excellent fitness center with all kinds of activities. Additionally, our hospital offers exceptional health and community care. Skiing, fishing, hunting, mountains, lakes, rivers, and the nearby ocean all add to the advantages of living in Farmington."

Despite its many positive features, Charles Murray can name a few drawbacks to life in this otherwise idyllic spot. "You're one-and-a-half hours from a significant airport," he notes. "And you should like winter or be able to get away for a break." Nevertheless, he believes Farmington to be an ideal retirement town. "It is easy to make connections here," he says. "If you are a newcomer, be sure to get involved in your church, town, and the many charitable committees or boards that need your help."

Rangeley *Franklin County*

At a Glance

Land Area: 41.64 square miles
Persons per Square Mile: 26
Population: 1,052
Median Age: 44.5 years
Neighboring Communities: Oquossoc, Rangeley Plantation, Dallas Plantation, Sandy River Plantation

Halfway between the equator and the North Pole, at an elevation of 1,547 feet, rests a tranquil region called the Rangeley Lakes. Mountains, lakes, rivers, and forest abound here and are home to a whole host of wildlife, from moose to eagles, trout to turtles. Outdoor recreation is the watchword in this western corner of the state, and residents enjoy fresh-air pursuits all year long. They fish and watch birds in the spring sunshine; canoe and bike as the summer sun sets; hunt and hike under a canopy of colorful leaves; and ski, snowshoe, and snowmobile on fresh blankets of snow.

The town of Rangeley is located on Rangeley Lake, one of seven lakes in this watershed hugging the New Hampshire border. With a year-round population of just over 1,000, Rangeley may contain more moose then men. And yet, despite the small pool of people, there's a surprising amount of activity here: civic groups and non-profit organizations, a busy arts association, a growing senior program, and lots of history to absorb and appreciate. Since retirees are drawn largely to Rangeley by outdoor pursuits, any cultural offerings the area provides are more of a bonus than a necessity.

"There is a large community of retired, but active, professional people with varied backgrounds and many shared values in Rangeley," says Don Palmer, who retired here in the 1980s and now heads both the Historical Society and the Guides and Sportsmen Association. He cites the town's informal style and welcoming attitude as two huge pluses to life in this quiet corner of Maine. Bob Silvia, a more recent retiree to Rangeley, agrees.

"Along with a wonderful book store, Rangeley has an amazing group of active retired people," notes the former company president. "It's the great outdoors, but still civilized."

While some who relocate to this rural neck of the woods may feel the lack of shopping centers, Rangeley's cute downtown does offer a fairly good range of small stores. A more serious challenge to daily life, especially for retirees, is the dearth of health care providers and facilities. Although there are primary physicians and some specialists, as well as a new rehabilitation and wellness center, residents needing a hospital must travel to Farmington's Franklin Memorial, a journey of some forty-plus miles. Residents do point out that the local ambulance service is excellent.

"Rangeley is a town where the active, outdoor lifestyle is celebrated," says a longtime resident. "It's a place where beauty is found in the wilderness and on the sparkling surface of ponds and lakes." Those with whom such sentiments resonate believe they have found a piece of pure Maine paradise in this pristine four-season community.

♠ WEATHER

Average Temperature (degrees Fahrenheit): January, 9.4; April, 36.1; July, 64.1; October, 41.9. **Average Annual Rainfall:** 43.24 inches. **Average Annual Snowfall:** 95.2 inches.

♠ TAXES

Property Tax Rate: $16.00 per $1,000 valuation. **Ratio to Current Market Value:** 87%.

♠ REAL ESTATE

Provided by James Eastlack, Morton and Furbish Real Estate (207-864-5777) **Older Housing Stock:** $130,000 to $140,000 in town; $235,000 to $275,000 out of town. **New Custom Construction:** $250,000 and up, depending on size and location. **Waterfront Locations:** $350,000 and up. **Rental Apartments:** $400 to $500/month.

> *Rangeley is a gem.*
>
> —James Eastlack,
> Morton and Furbish
> Real Estate

♠ RETIREMENT LIVING

Rangeley Townhouse Apartments (207-864-3986).

⚑ PUBLIC SAFETY

Crimes per 1,000 Population, 2000: 32.82. **Non-emergency Police**: 207-864-3579. **Non-emergency Fire**: 207-864-3326. **Emergency**: 911.

Says Police Chief Philip Weymouth, "Rangeley is one of the primary four-season resort towns in the state, a busy but peaceful place with a police force that works with its community to keep it safe so you can relax and enjoy yourself."

⚑ HEALTH CARE

Closest Hospitals: Franklin Memorial Hospital (207-778-6031, www.fchn.org) is a 70-bed, acute-care, community general hospital in Farmington, 43 miles away. Rangeley Region Health Center (207-864-3303; www.HealthReachCHC.org) provides basic medical care. The new Rangeley Region Rehabilitation and Wellness Pavillion provides state-of-the-art rehabilitation services and fitness programs (207-864-2900; www.rangeleyhealth.org). **Long-Term Care Facilities**: Edgewood Rehabilitation and Living Center (207-778-3386), 43 miles away.

⚑ CONTINUING EDUCATION

Senior College: Closest is Gold Leaf Institute at the University of Maine at Farmington (207-778-7063). Elderhostel programs are held at the Wilhelm Reich Museum (207-864-3443).

An art show held annually in Rangeley brings visitors from far and wide.

PHOTO COURTESY OF THE RANGELEY LAKES
CHAMBER OF COMMERCE

Colleges and Universities: Closest is the University of Maine at Farmington (207-778-7000). **Adult Education Programs**: Rangeley Adult Education Department (207-864-2028).

⚑ LIBRARY
Rangeley Public Library (207-864-5529; www.rangeleyme.com /library).

⚑ HISTORICAL SOCIETY
207-864-5647

⚑ SPECIFICALLY FOR SENIORS
The Town Office (207-864-3326) sponsors occasional trips for seniors; eligible seniors may receive discounted meals through a program held at Rangeley Townhouse Apartments (207-864-3986).

Rangeley Public Library
7 Lake Street, Rangeley

Hours:
Tuesday through Friday, 10:00 a.m. to 4:30 p.m.
Saturday, 10:00 a.m. to 2:00 p.m.

Rangeley Public Library was dedicated in 1909, and in 1959 a Children's Room was furnished on the second floor. In 1978, the library was honored by membership in the National Register of Historic Places, and in 2002, a community capital campaign raised funds for an addition of 5,700 square feet. New services include handicap access, a circulation desk, and a young-adult room, as well as areas for quiet reading and study, computer technology, and special collections. For more information, see www.rangeleyme.com/library.

Rangeley offers beautiful lakes and ponds for a quiet canoe ride. PHOTO COURTESY OF THE RANGELEY LAKES CHAMBER OF COMMERCE

♣ VOLUNTEERING

There are plenty of places to volunteer in Rangeley. The Friends of the Library, the Rangeley Lake Association, the Historical Society, the Rangeley Lakes Heritage Trust, and the Rangeley Friends of the Arts all welcome your help. Contact the Chamber of Commerce (800-685-2537) for more information.

♣ RECREATION

Golf: Mingo Springs (207-864-5021) has eighteen challenging and scenic holes. **Tennis Courts**: Lakeside Park has outdoor courts. **Parks**: Lakeside Park, Rangeley Lakes State Park. **Running/Walking/Biking**: Walking paths are found at the Wilhelm Reich Museum. Contact the Chamber of Commerce (800-685-2537) for a detailed map of hiking trails. **Fitness Classes**: Rangeley Wellness Center (207-864-2900). **Hunting/Fishing**: Call the Town Office for licenses at 207-864-3326.

Skiing: Cross-country trails are found at Rangeley Cross Country Ski Trails (207-864-4309) and Saddleback Ski Area (207-864-5671), where there are also forty alpine trails and five lifts.

♠ ENTERTAINMENT

Cinemas: Lakeside Theatre (207-864-5000). **Museums**: Wilhelm Reich was a physician-scientist whose scientific investigations led to his discovery of what he called orgone energy. His home in Rangeley is now a museum (207-864-3443). Rangeley Lakes Region Logging Museum (Box 154, Rangeley, ME 04970) celebrates an important North Woods industry. **Theaters**: Rangeley Friends of the Arts (www.rangeleyarts.com).

♠ NATURE

Hunter Cove Wildlife Sanctuary. Rangeley Lakes Heritage Trust (www.rlht.org) was founded in 1991 and has preserved more than 10,000 acres, including more than twenty miles of lake and river frontage, ten islands, and a 2,443-foot mountain.

♠ SHOPPING

A small supermarket is located right in Rangeley. The nearest mall is ninety miles away in Auburn. A number of small gift shops are located downtown, as are hardware and building supply stores, a real estate office, a pharmacy, and sporting goods stores.

♠ WHO LIVES HERE

Population: 1,052. **Median Age**: 44.5. **Percentage Age 62 and Older**: 24%. **Percentage with Bachelor's Degree**: 18.2%. **Percentage with Graduate or Professional Degree**: 8.5%. **Median Household Income**: $33,382. **Mean Retirement Income**: $19,282. **Per Capita Income**: $19,052.

♦ ESSENTIAL PHONE NUMBERS AND WEB SITES

Chamber of Commerce: 800-685-2537; www.rangeleymaine.com.
Town Office: 207-864-3326. **Voter and Vehicle Registration**: Town
Clerk's Department (207-864-3578). **Drivers' Licenses**: Closest
Motor Vehicle Office is in Mexico, a forty-five-minute drive away
(207-369-9921).

♦ LOCAL NEWS

Newspapers: *Rangeley Highlander* (207-864-3756), *Original Irregular* (207-265-2773). **Community Cable Station**: Channel 11. **Community
Internet Sites**: www.rangeleymaine.com and www.Rangeleynews.com.

♦ TRANSPORTATION

Bus: A van gives rides to seniors (207-864-3765). **Closest Airport**:
Portland or Bangor. **Taxi**: Rangeley Taxi (207-864-2343). **Traffic**:
Very light.

♦ DISTANCE TO OTHER CITIES

Portland, Me. 131.1 miles
Bangor, Me. 119.9 miles
Boston, Mass. 225.6 miles
New York, N.Y. 438.6 miles
Montreal, Quebec 194.8 miles
Quebec City, Quebec 175.8
miles

*The North Country Inn has four guest
rooms with views of lakes and mountains.*

PHOTO BY KAREN AND JERRY LEACH

⬥ JOBS

Rangeley is one of twenty-four communities and several unorganized territories in the Farmington Labor Market. Annual figures for the area in 2001 were: **Civilian Labor Force**: 17,080; **Employed**: 15,950; **Unemployed**: 1,130; **Unemployment Rate**: 6.6%.

⬥ UTILITIES

Electricity: Central Maine Power (800-750-4000). **Water**: Rangeley Water (207-864-5680). **Telephone**: Verizon (800-585-4466). **Cable TV**: Adelphia (800-336-9988). **Internet Service Providers**: TDS Telecom (888-483-7638), Megalink (207-336-2300).

⬥ PLACES OF WORSHIP

Faiths represented in the Rangeley Lakes area include Catholic, Baptist, Congregational, and Episcopal. The closest synagogues are located in Auburn; call the Jewish Federation (207-786-4201) for details.

⬥ EVENTS AND FESTIVALS

Small-town festivals take place throughout the year, including an Independence Day celebration in the Town Park, Logging Museum Festival Days and Parade in July, an annual August Art Show and Blueberry Festival, and the January Snowmobile Snodeo.

⬥ RESTAURANTS

Dining choices vary among 25 eateries, from the Rangeley Inn's Dining Room (207-864-3341), with its elegant fine dining; the Red Onion Restaurant on Main Street (207-864-5022), a casual spot featuring pizza, steaks, and soup; and the glassed-in dining room of the Country Club Inn (207 864-3831; www.countryclubinnrangeley.com) with its panoramic views.

⚴ LODGING

Cottages, camps, motels, hotels, inns, sporting camps—there are
many options for lodging in Rangeley. Here are a few choices:
North Country Inn B & B (207-864-2440; www.NorthCountryBB.com)
has four guest rooms with views of lakes and mountains. The
Rangeley Inn (207-864-3341; www.rangeleyinn.com) is a historic,
waterfront, country inn. The Country Club Inn (207 864-3831;
www.countryclubinnrangeley.com) has spectacular views and com-
fortable rooms.

⚴ WHAT THE LOCALS SAY

Bob Silvia retired here from Bolton, Massachusetts, because he loves
the outdoors. He'd taken vacations in Rangeley before, spending
leisurely days hunting, camping, and fishing in the cool, clear waters.
Although he had neither family nor friends in the area, he took the
plunge and bought a house for year-round living in Rangeley.

"Before moving here, my biggest question had to do with
medical care. What would I do if I needed it? Truthfully, it's still a
concern of mine."

Although Bob knew he'd take pleasure in the outdoor activities
Rangeley offered, he was surprised to discover a large pool of like-
minded people with whom to pursue them. "Everything I enjoy doing
is here, along with people to do it with," he says. He has found it
easy to become involved in local activities and has had no trouble
making connections with other residents.

To those thinking about moving, Bob gives this advice: "Anyone considering retirement here should spend nonvacation time in
town so that they have a real feel for the area. Rent a place for three
to six months before moving. That way, you'll know if Rangeley is
really for you."

▲▲▲

Midcoast

Sagadahoc and Lincoln Counties constitute Maine's Midcoast, an area stretching from the city of Bath to the town of Waldoboro. Sagadahoc is Maine's smallest county in area and includes beautiful coves and bays, notably Merrymeeting Bay, where five Maine rivers, including the Kennebec and Androscoggin, converge. Lincoln—where both of our midcoast towns are located—is a mix of coastal and inland towns and offshore islands like the artist colony of Monhegan

Lincoln County contains no cities, and the area's largest town is Waldoboro, settled around 1740 by German families who were brought to America by General Samuel Waldo. Profiled on the following pages are the midcoast towns of Boothbay Harbor and Damariscotta, two coastal hamlets with striking scenery, friendly residents, and lots of opportunities for volunteer involvement.

Boothbay Harbor is beautiful in all seasons. PHOTO BY STEPHEN RUBICAM

Boothbay Harbor *Lincoln County*

At a Glance

Land Area: 5.77 square miles
Persons per Square Mile: 409
Population: 2,334
Median Age: 48.3 years
Neighboring Communities: Boothbay, Southport, Edgecomb,
    Newcastle, Wiscasset

The Boothbay Harbor region is a seventeen-mile-long peninsula, about four miles wide, jutting into the Atlantic, bordered on the east by the Damariscotta River and on the west by the Sheepscot. This long arm of land, accessed from U.S. Route 1 by Route 27 South, is composed of four towns: Boothbay, Boothbay Harbor, Edgecomb, and Southport, an island connected to West Boothbay Harbor by a bridge. While the four towns together have a year-round population of less than 7,000, the number jumps to more than 50,000 in the summer months. Yes, this is prime Vacationland, complete with lobsters, taffy, trolleys, and seasonal traffic that can be, as one resident described it, "hideous" come July and August.

Boothbay Harbor's several fingers of land lie at the end of the peninsula. Surrounded as it is on three sides by water, the town has a strong and enduring marine heritage. This is one of the best-known boating centers in New England, a fact borne out by the many windjammers, lobster boats, fishing charters, and pleasure craft that ply the waters. More than twenty-five excursion boats visit nearby islands in the summer, heading out through Linekin Bay to the open water, while smaller craft paddle peacefully down the tidal rivers.

Boothbay Harbor's busy downtown is connected to East Boothbay by a picturesque footbridge across the Damariscotta River.

Routes 27 and 96 are the main thoroughfares, with 96 ending in the dramatic area known as Ocean Point. West Boothbay overlooks Spruce and Juniper Points and provides access to the neighboring island of Southport.

As a retirement destination, Boothbay Harbor has much to recommend it. Residents speak highly of St. Andrews Hospital, a twenty-bed, acute-care center, and its nonprofit retirement community, St. Andrews Village. Those who have relocated here aren't bored, especially during the warm-weather months, and note that larger towns with more cultural offerings (such as Brunswick) are only a short drive away. And community pride in the region is high: there's a gorgeous YMCA, new botanical gardens, and an active land trust with miles of mapped trails. Boothbay Harbor's many civic groups tend to welcome newcomers and are an excellent way both to help the community and make friends.

♦ WEATHER

Average Temperature (degrees Fahrenheit): January, 21.1; April, 43.6; July, 68.5; October, 48.1. **Average Annual Rainfall:** 45.23 inches. **Average Annual Snowfall:** 75.9 inches.

♦ TAXES

Property Tax Rate: $13.88 per $1,000 valuation. **Ratio to Current Market Value:** 100%.

♦ REAL ESTATE

Provided by Bruce Tindal, Tindal & Callahan Real Estate (207-633-6711)
Older Housing Stock: $150,000 to $795,000, depending on location. **New Custom Construction:** $395,000 to $895,000, depending on size and location. **Waterfront Locations:** $495,000 to $2,000,000. **Rental Apartments:** $500 to $1,000/month.

A cottage home in St. Andrews Village.

⬥ RETIREMENT LIVING

St. Andrews Village Retirement Community (207-633-0920; www
.standrewsvillage.com), a project of St. Andrews Hospital and
Healthcare Center, provides the full continuum of care, including
independent-living cottages and apartments.

⬥ PUBLIC SAFETY

Crimes per 1,000 Population, 2000: 32.23. **Non-emergency Police:**
207-633-2451. **Non-emergency Fire:** 207-633-2451. **Emergency:** 911.

Stephen Clark, Boothbay Harbor's chief of police, says, "This
is one of the safest communities in Maine. I attribute that to several
factors, including the spirit and character of the people in the Boothbay region; the neighbor-helping-neighbor atmosphere, which extends
to watching out for crimes and suspicious activity; the geography;
and the good work and dedication of law enforcement and public
safety in the area."

♣ HEALTH CARE

Closest Hospitals: St. Andrews Hospital and Healthcare Center (207-633-2121; www.standrewshealthcare.org) offers a twenty-four-hour emergency department, walk-in clinic, and surgical in- and out-patient services. **Clinics**: Boothbay Whole Health Medical Center (207-633-3535; www.wholehealth@gwi.net). **Long-Term Care Facilities**: St. Andrews Village (207-633-6996; www.standrewsvillage.com).

♣ CONTINUING EDUCATION

Senior College: Closest is Midcoast Senior College, located thirty-three miles away at University College of Bath/Brunswick (207-725-8620). **Adult Education Programs**: School Union 49 (207-633-3224).

♣ LIBRARY

Boothbay Harbor Memorial Library (207-633-3112; www.bmpl.lib.me.us).

♣ HISTORICAL SOCIETY

Boothbay Region Historical Society (207-633-0820).

> *With a warm coastal climate, easy access to boating, our YMCA, and great health care facilities, Boothbay Harbor is a wonderful place to retire.*
>
> —Bruce Tindal, Tindal & Callahan Real Estate

♣ SPECIFICALLY FOR SENIORS

Boothbay Region YMCA (207-633-2855) sponsors programs just for seniors. The Methodist Church has special events as well.

♣ VOLUNTEERING

Friends of the Library, Lincoln Arts Festival, and St. Andrews Hospital Auxiliary are just a few of the many organizations that welcome your help. Call the Chamber of Commerce (207-633-2353) for contact information.

Boothbay Harbor Memorial Library
4 Oak Street, Boothbay Harbor

Hours:
Tuesday, Thursday, Friday, and Saturday, 10:00 a.m. to 4:30 p.m.
Wednesday, 10:00 a.m. to 7:00 p.m.

Boothbay Harbor Memorial Library celebrated its eightieth year of service in 2003. Located in the heart of downtown Boothbay Harbor, the beautiful Greek Revival building is headed for much-needed expansion in the near future. A collection of 22,000 volumes includes a special Maine historical collection and the Lieutenant Tristram E. Farnham, U.S.N., Memorial Collection. The library offers a wide range of professional services, including interlibrary loan, book delivery to shut-ins, and public-access computers, and is known for its diverse cultural, educational, and arts-and-literature programs for patrons of all ages. For more information, visit www.bmpl.lib.me.us.

⚓ RECREATION

Golf: Boothbay Country Club is an eighteen-hole golf course offering challenging play for all levels of players (207-633-6085; www.boothbaycountryclub.com). **Tennis Courts**: By the high school. **Parks**: Barrett Park on Linekin Bay offers swimming, a playground, and picnic tables; Fisherman's Memorial Park on Atlantic Avenue overlooks the harbor. **Running/Walking/Biking**: Coastal Maine Botanical Gardens (207-633-4333) is a 128-acre preserve situated on 3,600 feet of shore frontage with gardens and trails. Damariscove Island (207-633-2353), the site of one of the earliest white settlements in America (1605), is a great spot to hike or go birdwatching. **Fitness Classes**: Boothbay Region YMCA (207-633-2855; www.brymca.com). **Hunting/Fishing**: Call the Town Office for licenses at 207-633-3672.

Skiing: Cross-country ski on the trails at the Botanical Gardens; closest downhill ski area is the Camden Snow Bowl (207-236-3438).

♣ ENTERTAINMENT

Cinemas: Harbor Theatre (207-633-0438). **Museums**: Boothbay Region Historical Society (207-633-0820) has seven display rooms containing artifacts and memorabilia that reflect the region's colonial and coastal origins. **Theaters**: Carousel Music Theatre (207-633-5297; www.boothbaydinnertheatre.com), Lincoln Arts Festival Association (207-563-3328; www.LincolnArtsFestival.org), Lincoln County Community Theatre (207-529-5977).

♣ NATURE

Boothbay Region Land Trust Preserve (208-633-4818) has eighteen miles of coastal and woodland trails. Also, visit Coastal Maine Botanical Gardens (207-633-4333).

♣ SHOPPING

In addition to taffy and ice cream, you can buy "real" food in Boothbay Harbor. A large supermarket is located on Route 27, and there are smaller stores, including a delicatessen, on both sides of the harbor. Many of Boothbay Harbor's downtown stores sell tourist-related items. Hardware and discount stores are found by nearby Route 1; the nearest mall is located in Portland.

♣ WHO LIVES HERE

Population: 2,334. **Median Age**: 48.3. **Percentage Age 62 and Older**: 29.7%. **Percentage with Bachelor's Degree**: 18.2%. **Percentage with Graduate or Professional Degree**: 12.1%. **Median Household Income**: $35,000. **Mean Retirement Income**: $17,703. **Per Capita Income**: $21,146.

▲ ESSENTIAL PHONE NUMBERS AND WEB SITES

Chamber of Commerce: 207-633-2353; www.boothbayharbor.com. **Town Office**: 207-633-3672. **Voter and Vehicle Registration**: Town Clerk's Department (207-633-3672). **Drivers' Licenses**: Motor Vehicle Office in Topsham (207-725-6520).

▲ LOCAL NEWS

Newspapers: *The Boothbay Register* (877-500-6397). **Community Cable Station**: Channel 5. **Community Internet Sites**: www .boothbayharboron-line.com.

▲ TRANSPORTATION

Bus: Closest is in Wiscasset. **Tours**: F. L. Rice Taxi and Harbor Shuttle (877-381-7423). **Closest Airport**: Portland. **Limo Service**: Harbor Limousine (866-998-9998). **Taxi**: F. L. Rice Taxi and Harbor Shuttle (877-381-7423). **Train**: Closest stop is in Portland. **Traffic**: Very congested in the summer.

▲ DISTANCE TO OTHER CITIES

Portland, Me. 57.6 miles
Bangor, Me. 94.9 miles
Boston, Mass. 168.9 miles
New York, N.Y. 373.7 miles
Montreal, Quebec 281.8 miles
Quebec City, Quebec 253.1 miles

▲ JOBS

Boothbay Harbor is one of ten communities in the Boothbay Harbor Labor Market. Annual figures for the area in 2001 were: **Civilian Labor Force**: 9,400; **Employed**: 9,170; **Unemployed**: 240; **Unemployment Rate**: 2.5%.

⚓ UTILITIES

Electricity: Central Maine Power (800-750-4000). **Water:** 207-633-4723. **Telephone:** Verizon (800-585-4466). **Cable TV:** Adelphia (800-336-9988). **Internet Service Providers:** Great Works Internet (877-494-4932), Midcoast Internet Solutions (207-563-8563).

⚓ PLACES OF WORSHIP

The Boothbay Harbor Region is home to many churches, including the Christian Science Society, the First United Methodist, and the Congregational. The closest synagogue is Beth Israel, located in Bath.

⚓ EVENTS AND FESTIVALS

Boothbay in Bloom and Windjammer Days take place in June, an annual Fishermen's Festival is in April, a Jazz Weekend happens in July, and a Fall Foliage Festival is in October.

⚓ RESTAURANTS

There are scores of great places to eat in Boothbay Harbor. Here are a few choices: Biscotti Café (207-633-3464), Blue Moon Café (207-633-2349), Boat House Bistro (207-633-7300), Boothbay Harbor Inn (207-633-6302).

⚓ LODGING

There are dozens of places to spend the night. A few to try are the oceanfront Sur la Mer Inn (800-791-2026; www.surlamerinn.com); the Footbridge Inn, a sea captain's home on the waterfront (888-633-9965); and the Kenniston Hill Inn (800-992-2915).

⚓ WHAT THE LOCALS SAY

Nearly forty years of summers spent in the Boothbay Harbor region convinced Barbara and Ray Ripley that the area was where they wanted to retire. "Because of our summertime experience, we knew what life was like here. We knew tradespeople and other year-rounders from other states. Our youngest son, Peter, married a girl from a fifth-generation summer family, and they live here as well. So this was the place for us."

In 2002, the couple moved into a cottage at St. Andrews Village, where they appreciate a central location as well as attentive staff. "The management is most helpful in arranging visits to interesting museums, educational lectures, and places of interest in Augusta and elsewhere," notes Ray. He says that they are involved in activities "to whatever degree we choose to be. There's a great small-town feeling of camaraderie in Boothbay Harbor."

The Ripleys have not found any surprises or disappointments in their new home, and they feel they can describe the ideal Boothbay Harbor retiree: "He or she should enjoy four-season weather or, failing that, become a 'snow bird.' It doesn't hurt at all if one enjoys pretty scenery, Maine's shoreline charm, and the ocean's fascinating moods."

Boats on their moorings in Boothbay Harbor. PHOTO BY TOM CARBONE

Damariscotta
Lincoln County

At a Glance

Land Area: 12.41 square miles
Persons per Square Mile: 164
Population: 2,041
Median Age: 48 years
Neighboring Communities: Newcastle, Nobleboro, Bremen, Bristol

The name Damariscotta derives from an Abenaki Indian word meaning "plenty of alewives." These fish, closely related to herring, have migrated annually to this area since prehistoric times and still arrive in abundance each spring. The tongue-twisting appellation is frequently used in this corner of midcoast Maine; it graces a large lake in nearby Jefferson and Nobleboro as well as the river that flows from the lake to the ocean. Finally, Damariscotta is also the name of the riverside town, incorporated in 1847, that was once one of New England's most important shipbuilding centers and is today a quaint yet vibrant community.

Damariscotta and neighbor Newcastle are called the "Twin Villages." Located on either side of the Damariscotta River's head, twelve miles from the ocean and linked by a bridge, the towns comprise the trading center for Lincoln County. Both were included in the Pemaquid Patent of 1629 and contain many historic houses and buildings of the colonial period, some of which, such as the Chapman Hall House in Damariscotta, are open for tours. Together, the towns share a more ancient history: shell heaps, or "middens," dating back at least 2,400 years are found along the river, reminders of oyster feasts enjoyed by Indians who summered in this spot long ago.

Unlike some of Maine's coastal villages, the hub of Damariscotta is not bisected by busy U.S. Route 1. Instead, an offshoot, Business Route 1 North, winds across the river and becomes Damariscotta's

Main Street. This happy arrangement greatly reduces the seasonal traffic headaches for both tourists and residents and helps to keep the downtown's village character intact.

Even with its busy little downtown, Damariscotta has a quiet, rural feel about it that greatly appeals to some retirees. Stately white churches, graceful old homes, carefully tended flower gardens, and the natural beauty of hills, forest, fields, wetlands, brooks, tidal river, and bog blend in a landscape that is pure small New England town. Add to these scenic charms excellent facilities such as Miles Memorial Hospital and the new Skidompha Public Library, and the resulting combination is pretty hard to resist. Nearby attractions such as Pemaquid Point, site of a lovely crescent beach and historic lighthouse, and the Rachel Carson Salt Pond Preserve on the shores of Muscongus Bay only add to the magic of Damariscotta.

⚑ WEATHER

Average Temperature (degrees Fahrenheit): January, 21.1; April, 43.6; July, 68.5; October, 48.1. **Average Annual Rainfall:** 45.23 inches. **Average Annual Snowfall:** 75.9 inches.

⚑ TAXES

Property Tax Rate: $19.30 per $1,000 valuation. **Ratio to Current Market Value:** 95%.

⚑ REAL ESTATE

Provided by Bill Byrnes, Newcastle Square Real Estate (207-563-3435)
Older Housing Stock: $125,000 to $295,000, depending on location. **New Custom Construction:** $180,000 to $300,000 and up, depending on size and loca-

> *Damariscotta's charms include natural beauty, great facilities, and village-style living where people know each other.*
>
> —Bill Byrnes, Newcastle Square Real Estate

tion. **Waterfront Locations**: $1 million. **Riverfront Lots**: $200,000.
Rental Apartments: $500 to $600/month.

♠ RETIREMENT LIVING

Schooner Cove (207-563-5523; www.mileshealthcare.org/schooner),
a project of Miles Health Care, offers independent-living apartments
that can be purchased or rented as well as amenities such as a waterfront location, dining room, and housekeeping. Chase Point, also
under the Miles Health Care banner, offers twenty-four assisted-living
apartments, some of which are in a separate memory-impairment
residence. The Lincoln Home in Newcastle offers assisted- and independent-living apartments (207-563-3350; www.lincoln-home.org).

♠ PUBLIC SAFETY

Crimes per 1,000 Population, 2000: 41.36. **Non-emergency Police**:
207-563-1909. **Non-emergency Fire**: 207-563-8286. **Emergency**: 911.

Sergeant Thomas Hoepner, Damariscotta's acting chief of
police, says, "As the business hub for Lincoln County, this is a great
place to live and work. Our department works hard to keep the town
safe as well."

♠ HEALTH CARE

Closest Hospitals: Miles Memorial Hospital (207-563-1234) offers
thirty-two acute-care beds. **Clinics**: Miles Health Care Center at
Miles Memorial Hospital. **Long-Term Care Facilities**: Cove's Edge
(207-563-4600) provides rehabilitation and long-term care and is
part of the Miles Health Care.

♠ CONTINUING EDUCATION

Senior College: Several courses are held at Schooner Cove; call
800-286-1594 for information. **Adult Education Programs**: Lincoln

Academy (207-563-3596), Round Top Center for the Arts (207-563-1507).

⬥ LIBRARY
Skidompha Public Library (207-563-5513).

⬥ HISTORICAL SOCIETY
Pemaquid Historical Association, Box 4000-314, Damariscotta, ME 04543.

Skidompha Public Library
P.O. Box 70
184 Main Street, Damariscotta

Hours:
Tuesday, Wednesday, and Friday, 9:00 a.m. to 5:00 p.m.
Thursday, 9:00 a.m. to 7:00 p.m.
Saturday, 9:00 a.m. to 1:00 p.m.

The name Skidompha dates back to 1905 and is an acronym built with initials from founding members' names. In 1998, a gift from internationally acclaimed author and illustrator Barbara Cooney Porter, a local resident, sparked a capital campaign for a new library building. In three years, over $3.2 million was raised, principally from local residents and businesses, and in 2001, the new building opened. Today, the collection numbers about 25,000 items, supplemented by four public-access computers and associated hardware. Computer training for adults, an automated circulation system, strong genealogy and local history collections, and an active children's wing and programs are among Skidompha's hallmarks. For more information, see www.skidompha.org.

♠ SPECIFICALLY FOR SENIORS

The Central Lincoln County YMCA (207-563-3477) offers activities for seniors. Senior Spectrum (800-639-1553) is a clearinghouse for a wide range of programs.

♠ VOLUNTEERING

The Miles Memorial Hospital League (207-563-1234), Newcastle–Damariscotta Women's Club (207-563-2260), the Lincoln County Animal Shelter (207-882-9677), and the Damariscotta River Association (207-563-1393) all welcome your help.

♠ RECREATION

Golf: Wawenock Country Club has nine holes plus a driving range in nearby Walpole (207-563-3938). Sheepscot Links Golf Course (207-549-5750) has nine challenging holes in the Sheepscot River Valley. **Tennis Courts:** At Lincoln Academy. **Parks:** Colonial Pemaquid State Park features Fort William Henry. **Running/Walking/Biking:** The Damariscotta River Association has miles of trails for walking or running (207-563-1393). **Fitness Classes:** Central Lincoln County YMCA (207-563-3477; www.clcymca.com). **Hunting/Fishing:** Call the Town Office for licenses at 207-563-5168. **Skiing:** Cross-country ski on trails at the Salt Bay Heritage Center (207-563-1393). Closest downhill ski area is the Camden Snow Bowl (207-236-3438).

♠ ENTERTAINMENT

Cinemas: Lincoln County Community Theatre (207-563-3424). **Museums:** Harrington Meeting House contains a small museum of old photographs, clothing, and books. The adjoining cemetery has gravestones of historical interest. Chapman Hall House, built in 1754, has period furnishings, an herb garden, and eighteenth-century rose bushes. **Theaters:** Round Top Center for the Arts (207-563-1507), Lincoln County Community Theatre (207-563-3424).

The Round Top Center for the Arts in Damariscotta. PHOTO BY GENETTA MCLEAN

⬥ NATURE

The Damariscotta River Association, based at the Salt Bay Heritage Center, is working to preserve the area's scenic, cultural, and natural history; exhibits and trails on site (207-563-1393; www.lincoln .midcoast.com). Rachel Carson Salt Pond Preserve, a one-quarter-acre tidal pool, is on the shores of Muscongus Bay and was a favorite spot of the famous environmentalist.

⬥ SHOPPING

Supermarkets and grocery stores are located right in Damariscotta, as are useful small stores including a hardware store, pharmacy, fish market, and Maine Coast Café and Book Shop (207-563-3207). The nearest mall is in Portland, although Damariscotta boasts the original Renys Department Store, a Maine icon.

⬥ WHO LIVES HERE

Population: 2,041. **Median Age**: 48. **Percentage Age 62 and Older**: 33.4%. **Percentage with Bachelor's Degree**: 23.4%. **Percentage with**

Graduate or Professional Degree: 10.5%. Median Household Income: $36,187. Mean Retirement Income: $17,424. Per Capita Income: $23,146.

▲ ESSENTIAL PHONE NUMBERS AND WEB SITES

Chamber of Commerce: 207-563-8340; www.damariscottaregion .com. Town Office: 207-563-5168. Voter and Vehicle Registration: Town Clerk's Department (207-563-5168). Drivers' Licenses: Motor Vehicle Office in Topsham (207-725-6520). Newcomers Organization: The Friendly Folks (207-563-3568).

▲ LOCAL NEWS

Newspapers: *Lincoln County News* (207-563-3171; www.lincoln .midcoast.com), Lincoln *County Weekly* (207-563-5006). Community Cable Station: Channel 4. Community Internet Sites: www .damariscottaregion.com, www.damariscotta.com.

▲ TRANSPORTATION

Bus: Concord Trailways (800-639-8080) stops in Damariscotta and continues south to Boston. Tours: Hardy Boat Cruises (207-677-6026) offers lighthouse, puffin, and seal trips. Closest Airport: Portland or Bangor. Limo Service: Portland Limo (800-585-3589), Midcoast Limo (207-937-2424). Train: Closest stop is in Portland. Traffic: Usually light; moderate in season.

▲ DISTANCE TO OTHER CITIES

Portland, Me. 53.1 miles
Bangor, Me. 77.8 miles
Boston, Mass. 164.4 miles
New York, N.Y. 369.2 miles
Montreal, Quebec 276.2 miles
Quebec City, Quebec 247.5 miles

↟ JOBS

Damariscotta is one of ten communities in the Boothbay Harbor Labor Market. Annual figures for the area in 2001 were: **Civilian Labor Force**: 9,400; **Employed**: 9,170; **Unemployed**: 240; **Unemployment Rate**: 2.5%.

↟ UTILITIES

Electricity: Central Maine Power (800-750-4000). **Water**: Great Salt Bay Sanitation Department (207-563-5105). **Telephone**: Verizon (800-585-4466). **Cable TV**: Adelphia (800-336-9988). **Internet Service Providers**: Midcoast Internet Solutions (207-563-8563), Tidewater Telecom (207-563-9911).

↟ PLACES OF WORSHIP

The Damariscotta region has nearly two dozen churches of various faiths, including the historic St. Patrick's in Newcastle. Not only is the

The Maine Coast Book Shop Cafe on Main Street has books, magazines, and stationery. PHOTO BY TRUDY PRICE

structure the oldest surviving Catholic church in New England, but it contains a bell cast by Paul Revere.

♠ EVENTS AND FESTIVALS

Events that occur in the Damariscotta region include the May Tulip Festival, a July Piano Festival, the August Antique Show, and the L.O.R.E. (Lakes, Ocean, Rivers, Environment) Fest in September.

♠ RESTAURANTS

Try the seafood and chowders at King Eider's Pub (207-563-6008) on Elm Street in town, sample the fare at Rogue River Food & Supply (207-563-2992), or journey to Edgecomb to the Sheepscot River Inn and Restaurant (207-882-7748).

LODGING

The Oak Gables B & B has five rooms and is open all year (207-563-1476; www.oakgablesbandb.com), while the Mandalay B & B (207-563-2260) has three cozy rooms. Nearby Newcastle offers more lodging options such as the classic Newcastle Inn (800-832-8669; www.newcastleinn.com).

♠ WHAT THE LOCALS SAY

Marilen and David Plumer moved into Schooner Cove after living in Damariscotta for several years. "When we first came, in 1986, we found the area so appealing, both because of its beauty and the large number of retirees here."

The couple cites Damariscotta's friendliness as one of the biggest advantages to life here. "So many people are 'from away' and are eager to make new friends. It's easy to get involved in local activities and simple to drive around the area."

A downside to living in this part of Maine is the distance from large shopping centers. "We have to drive more than twenty-five miles to bigger stores sometimes," Marilen notes. Nevertheless, the couple decided to stay in Damariscotta, settling into the retirement community three years ago.

"We had no concerns about living at Schooner Cove because we had visited many times. Everything is even better than we'd hoped, and we've made many new friends." Marilen Plumer advises anyone considering one of Maine's retirement villages to make several trips at different times of the year. "Do check out our area," she says, "as it has so much to offer."

▲▲▲

Penobscot Bay

Sweeping vistas of Penobscot Bay, dotted with
islands both populated and not, mark the eastern borders of
Knox and Waldo Counties. Established in 1860, Knox is Maine's
youngest county, and is named for General Henry Knox, George
Washington's secretary of war during the American Revolution. A
replica of his home, Montpelier, is in the coastal town of Thomaston.
The county's largest city is Rockland, an eclectic mix of working
waterfront and upscale downtown, home to about 8,000 people. In
recent years Rockland and several other towns in the Penobscot Bay
region have experienced growth due to the expansion of the credit-
card bank MBNA and the area's rising popularity as a year-round
community.

Waldo County's largest community and the area's only city is
Belfast. By and large, this county is a mixture of coastal towns like
Lincolnville and Searsport, famous for its sea captains' homes, and
small inland communities, some with patriotic names like Liberty,
Freedom, and Unity. Waldo County is also home to the tony island
community of Islesboro, reachable by a twenty-minute ferry ride
from the mainland.

The towns profiled in the Penobscot Bay region are Camden,
Islesboro, and Belfast. Each offers a distinct lifestyle, and yet all are
home to fine sailing grounds, caring residents, and small-town charm.
Common to all three towns are views of the Camden Hills, a ridge
of mountains that stretches along the coast, affording sweeping
views of the bay and islands. Mount Megunticook, part of Camden
Hills State Park, is, at 1,300 feet, the second tallest mountain on
the Eastern Seaboard.

Camden *Knox County*

At a Glance

Land Area: 17.79 square miles
Persons per Square Mile: 295
Population: 5,254
Median Age: 47 years
Neighboring Communities: Rockport, Lincolnville, Hope, Appleton

Camden, the most popular tourist town between Boothbay Harbor and Bar Harbor, nestles at the foot of the Camden Hills and along island-dotted Penobscot Bay. U.S. Route 1 goes straight through the center of town, winding its way past Camden Hills State Park and on to Lincolnville and Belfast. Just two miles south is the town of Rockport, once a part of Camden but now just a very good neighbor. Both communities enjoy lovely deepwater harbors that fill with colorful sailboats—including the majestic schooners called windjammers— come spring. While Rockport's small center is notable for its quiet, residential feel and relative lack of commercial activity, Camden's brick-fronted shops and restaurants bustle nearly year-round, the pace becoming somewhat frenetic at the height of tourist season.

For centuries, this part of Maine has been known for its incomparable sailing, and Camden boasts one of the few five-star harbors in the state. Recently, however, the area has gained recognition for its cultural offerings as well. Both Camden and Rockport have renovated opera houses that showcase dramatic and musical events, as well as a new auditorium at the regional high school that regularly hosts the Portland Symphony Orchestra and other performances. Local galleries, including the Center for Maine Contemporary Art in Rockport, display the work of painters, potters, and sculptors, while the Farnsworth Art Museum in nearby Rockland fills seven galleries with American work, ranging from the eighteenth century to the present day. Residents can see an opera, learn Russian at the Penobscot School, or discuss global issues at an annual international public affairs conference. Seniors here are an energetic bunch, with many of the town's organizations wholly or partly run by volunteers in their older years. As more than one retiree has pointed out, there's no shortage of things to do.

As with many Maine communities, outdoor pursuits play an important role in Camden. Summer brings boats of all shapes to the lakes, rivers, and bay, as well as hikers to the hills that rise like sentinels around the town. Fall is hunting season and time to don blaze orange when walking along rural routes. Winter is unpredictable along the coast: snow inspires residents to visit the town-owned ski area, the Snow Bowl, where breathtaking views of the ocean's blue waters are in stark contrast to the white-capped Camden Hills. Spring means mud and pesky black flies, as it does in nearly all of Maine.

The Penobscot Bay area is served by a hospital with a twenty-four-hour emergency room and a good contingent of specialists on call. A new retirement community, affiliated with Penobscot Bay Medical Center, offers assisted- as well as independent-living options, and a well-respected long-term care center—Windward Gardens—offers respite care for brief or extended stays. A new YMCA is quickly becoming the hub of social activity in the winter months, as is a new skating-and-tennis center in nearby West Rockport.

Skiers learn the basics at the Camden Snow Bowl. PHOTO BY BEN MAGRO

"We love that seven days a week we can get fresh croissants at 7 a.m., or the best hot bagels north of New York City," say Jay and Meredith Scheck. "When all else fails, a walk down to the harbor, no matter what the season, clears the mind and heals the soul."

⚑ WEATHER

Average Temperature (degrees Fahrenheit): January, 25.9; April, 42.7; July, 68.2; October, 48.4. **Average Annual Rainfall:** 46 inches. **Average Annual Snowfall:** 40 inches.

⚑ TAXES

Property Tax Rate: $18.06 per $1,000 valuation. **Ratio to Current Market Value:** 90%.

⚑ REAL ESTATE

Provided by Scott Horty, Camden Real Estate Company (207-236-6171)
Older Housing Stock: $150,000 to $450,000, depending on location. **New Custom Construction:** $200,000 and up, depending on size and location. **Waterfront Locations:** $500,000 and up. **Water-View Homes:** $350,000 and up. **Riverfront Lots:** $80,000 to $150,000. **Rental Apartments:** $600 to $900/month.

⚑ RETIREMENT LIVING

Completed in 2002, Quarry Hill (207-230-6116) offers independent- and assisted-living options in cottages and apartments on twenty-six acres. Camden Gardens (207-236-0154) has eight independent-living apartments and two cottages. In nearby Rockland, Bartlett Woods (207-594-2745) offers rental units to 57 residents.

⚑ PUBLIC SAFETY

Crimes per 1,000 Population, 2000: 14.15. **Non-emergency Police:** 207-236-3030. **Non-emergency Fire:** 207-236-7950. **Emergency:** 911.

Chief of Police Phillip Roberts says, "We are fortunate to live in a beautiful area but even more fortunate to be blessed with the wonderful community atmosphere that surrounds us. We at the Camden Police Department are proud to be a part of it."

♣ HEALTH CARE

Closest Hospitals: Penobscot Bay Medical Center in Rockport (207-596-8000) offers a twenty-four-hour emergency room along with comprehensive medical, surgical, psychiatric, cardiac, and cancer care. **Long-Term Care Facilities**: Windward Gardens (207-236-4197; www.sandyriverhealth.com) offers assisted living including extended care.

♣ CONTINUING EDUCATION

Senior College: Coastal Senior College, at University College at Thomaston (207-354-6906). **Colleges and Universities**: Nearby Rockport College (207-236-8581; www.rockportcollege.edu) has degree programs in photography, film, and creative writing. A branch of the University of Maine is in Thomaston, twelve miles south of Camden (800-286-1594). **Adult Education Programs**: Courses are held at the new Camden Hills Regional High School (207-236-7800). The Penobscot School (207-594-1084) is a nonprofit center for language learning.

♣ LIBRARY

Camden Public Library (207-236-3440).

♣ HISTORICAL SOCIETY

Camden–Rockport Historical Society (207-236-2257).

♣ SPECIFICALLY FOR SENIORS

Camden does not have a senior center, but Quarry Hill (207-230-6116) offers monthly senior programming open to the public.

The Camden Public Library sits at the head of Harbor Park. PHOTO BY MARK HASKELL

Camden Public Library
55 Main Street, Camden

Hours:
Monday through Friday, 9:30 a.m. to 5:00 p.m.
(Tuesday and Thursday until 8:00 p.m.)
Sunday, 1:00 to 5:00 p.m.

Camden Public Library, on the National Register of Historic Places, opened June 1, 1928. In 1996, the Centennial Wing, built beneath the library lawn, was completed. This $3 million expansion includes a large Children's Room, a community meeting space, and computer workstations, and also houses the main collection. The original library building has been restored as a quiet reading room. Periodicals and newspapers are available as well as Maine and rare book collections. Other features include the Edna St. Vincent Millay Collection. For more information, see www.camden.lib.me.com.

The new Penobscot Bay YMCA (207-236-3375) is a gathering place for active retirees.

⚴ VOLUNTEERING

Located in Camden, the Make-A-Wish Foundation (207-236-3171) welcomes volunteers, as does the Camden Public Library (207-236-3440) and the Camden–Rockport–Lincolnville Chamber of Commerce (207-236-4404).

⚴ RECREATION

Golf: Goose River Golf Course (207-236-8488) is a public course offering nine challenging holes. The Samoset Resort (207-594-2511) is an eighteen-hole public course on Penobscot Bay. **Tennis Courts**: Outside courts are located at the Camden Snow Bowl (207-236-3438) and Rockport Recreation Park (207-236-9648); indoor tennis takes place at the Midcoast Recreation Center (207-236-9400; www .midcoastrec.com). **Parks**: Camden Village Green; Harbor Hill Park; and Camden Hills State Park. **Running/Walking/Biking**: a new walking path along Union Street leads from the Camden–Rockport arch to Rockport Village. **Fitness Classes**: Penobscot Bay YMCA (207-236-3375), Optimum Performance (207-236-0844). **Horses/Riding**: Lily Hill Farm (207-236-2504). **Hunting/Fishing**: Call the Town Office for licenses at 207-236-3353. **Skiing**: Residents cross-country ski at the Megunticook Golf Course in Rockport and at Lincolnville's Tanglewood 4-H Camp; Camden's downhill ski area with ten trails is the Snow Bowl (207-236-3438).

⚴ ENTERTAINMENT

Cinemas: The Bayview Street Cinema (207-236-8722). **Museums**: Conway Homestead–Cramer Museum (207-236-2257) is an eighteenth-century restored farmhouse, barn, and sugarhouse. The Owls Head Transportation Museum (207-584-4418) is in nearby Owls

Head. **Art Museums**: The Center for Maine Contemporary Art (207-236-2875) is in Rockport village, and features the work of contemporary Maine artists. The Farnsworth Museum in Rockland (207-596-6457) has an exceptional collection of American art from all eras. **Theaters**: Camden Opera House (207-236-7963; www .camdenoperahouse.com) is a beautifully renovated space that houses the Camden Civic Theatre (207-236-2281) as well as other performers. **Music**: Bay Chamber Concerts (207-236-2823) and Maine Grand Opera Company (207-230-1200) offer shows throughout the year.

⚑ NATURE

Right in town, Merryspring Horticultural Park offers sixty-six quiet acres with four miles of walking trails and a ten-acre arboretum (207-236-9400).

⚑ SHOPPING

Small grocery stores are scattered around town; a good-sized supermarket straddles the Camden–Rockport line. Rockland has two large supermarkets as well as a few department stores. The nearest malls are in Bangor and Portland. Camden's downtown is home to a number of small specialty stores, many of which are open year-round.

⚑ WHO LIVES HERE

Population: 5,254. **Median Age**: 47. **Percentage Age 62 and Older**: 26.6%. **Percentage with Bachelor's Degree**: 28.1%. **Percentage with Graduate or Professional Degree**: 15.8%. **Median Household Income**: $39,877. **Mean Retirement Income**: $15,653. **Per Capita Income**: $26,126.

⚑ ESSENTIAL PHONE NUMBERS AND WEB SITES

Chamber of Commerce: 207-236-4404; www.camdenme.org. **Town Office**: 207-236-3353; www.town.camden.me.us). **Voter and Vehicle**

Camden offers beautiful hiking in Camden Hills State Park. PHOTO BY GINI MCKAIN

Registration: Town Clerk's Department (207-236-3353). **Drivers' Licenses**: Motor Vehicle Office in Rockland (207-596-2255). **Newcomers Organization**: Friendly Folks (207-236-4219).

▲ LOCAL NEWS

Newspapers: *Camden Herald* (207-236-8511; www.camdenherald.com). **Community Cable Station**: Channel 9. **Community Internet Sites**: www.villagesoup.com, www.camdenme.org, www.town.camden.me.us.

▲ TRANSPORTATION

Bus: Concord Trailways (800-639-3317; www.concordtrailways.com). **Closest Airport**: Knox County Airport in Owls Head. **Limo Service**: Mid-Coast Limousine (207-236-2424; www.midcoastlimo.com).

Train: Amtrak's Downeaster, in Portland. **Traffic**: Downtown is very busy in summer months; fairly quiet the rest of the year.

♠ DISTANCE TO OTHER CITIES
Portland, Me. 81.2 miles
Bangor, Me. 54.1 miles
Boston, Mass. 192.6 miles
New York, N.Y. 397.4 miles
Montreal, Quebec 286.9 miles
Quebec City, Quebec 245.8 miles

♠ JOBS
Camden is one of eighteen communities and one organized territory in the Rockland Labor Market. Annual figures for the area in 2001 were: **Civilian Labor Force**: 23,480; **Employed**: 22,810; **Unemployed**: 670; **Unemployment Rate**: 2.8%.

♠ UTILITIES
Electricity: Central Maine Power (800-750-4000). **Water**: Consumers Maine Water Company (207-236-8428). **Telephone**: Verizon (800-585-4466). **Cable TV**: Adelphia (800-336-9988). **Internet Service Providers**: Midcoast Internet Solutions (207-594-8277; www .midcoast.com).

♠ PLACES OF WORSHIP
About a dozen churches dot Camden and Rockport, including the historic Congregational and Baptist churches. The closest synagogue is Adas Yoshuron, in Rockland.

♠ EVENTS AND FESTIVALS
Numerous festivals take place throughout the year, including Saints and Spirits Weekend in March, annual Arts and Crafts Festivals in

July and October, and Christmas-by-the-Sea in December. Rockland is home to the colorful Maine Lobster Festival, held in August, and a popular Blues Festival in July.

▲ RESTAURANTS

Dining choices abound in this part of Maine. Downtown Camden has dockside dining, friendly pub-type eateries, and even a few ethnic choices. For lunch, try Boynton-McKay, a historic pharmacy downtown, or the Bagel Café, in a renovated mill building; for dinner, give Frogwater Café, The Waterfront, or Peter Ott's a try.

▲ LODGING

There are dozens of places to stay in Camden, from trim bed-and-breakfasts such as Blackberry Inn (207-236-6060) to convenient lodgings such as the in-town Lord Camden Inn (207-236-4325) and Best Western Riverhouse (207-236-0500).

▲ WHAT THE LOCALS SAY

"We purchased our home in 1999 after a week spent with a realtor looking at available homes in our price range between Belfast and Rockland," say Meredith and Jay Scheck of Camden. The Schecks knew the area: they'd transported their daughter to a nearby girls' camp every summer for ten years. "These visits introduced us to the area, and over time fostered our desire to spend time here in retirement. Our love of Maine was cemented in a week-long windjammer cruise that we took about a decade ago, and our daughter's love of Maine led her to go to Colby College in Waterville."

> *My clients retire here for the richness of life, including an abundance of culture, dining opportunities, outdoor activities, and the chance to become part of a great community.*
>
> —Scott Horty, Camden Real Estate Company

The Schecks bought a small Victorian home, built in 1895, that is two blocks from the harbor. "We wanted an in-town setting with next-door neighbors and easy walking access to shopping, the library, and restaurants. Beyond these personal considerations, we also think there is not a more beautiful Maine coastal town, or a more picturesque harbor, than Camden." While the Schecks' home is a year-round one, they presently divide their time between Maine and Florida, where they have family.

Meredith and Jay had few concerns before purchasing their home. "Naturally, we hoped that over time we would be successful in establishing a circle of friends. While this can be harder to do in an established community, as opposed to moving into a retirement community, for the most part it has worked out well. One other concern related to the old home that we bought, which required significant repair and restoration. We worried about how difficult it would be to find good people to do the work."

While their experience in Camden has been "overwhelmingly positive," the Schecks have found a few negatives. As they feared, some contractors here are hard to pin down and schedule. Getting a mooring in Camden harbor has proved difficult, and "big-box" shopping is at least forty-five miles away. Real estate prices have risen dramatically in the past few years, "and the tourist traffic through downtown in July and August is daunting!"

Despite these concerns, the Schecks are happy with their choice. "We wanted a community with people of all ages, working and not. Camden is just the kind of vibrant small town that we were looking for."

▲▲▲

Islesboro
Waldo County

At a Glance

Land Area: 14.25 square miles
Persons per Square Mile: 43
Population: 603
Median Age: 45.9 years
Neighboring Communities: Lincolnville, Belfast, Camden

Islesboro, a ten-mile-long stretch of land in Penobscot Bay, is a year-round island community, three miles out to sea and reachable by a state-operated and -subsidized ferry from Lincolnville Beach. The year-round population of about 600 swells to a figure several times that in July and August, when "summer people" arrive to fill the cottages and homes—some of them palatial—that ring the island. Only twenty minutes by water from the mainland, Islesboro remains largely unchanged from the turn of the century, when it was known as a grand, but informal, resort colony. Its two communities are Dark Harbor, where the Town Office and library are located, and Pripet, a thriving neighborhood of fishermen and boat builders.

Despite the presence of famous summer residents that include John Travolta, Islesboro has not been commercialized, and for all of its exclusivity, the residents are surprisingly friendly. Much of the island workforce is involved in the construction, maintenance, and land management business, with a fair share also working in marine trades and fishing. There are three busy boatyards as well as an active fleet of thirty or so lobster boats. Destinations include a small Sailor's Memorial Museum, a few grocery stores, and several seasonal shops, but for everything else, residents hop on either the *Margaret Chase Smith* or a local water taxi for the three-mile ride to the mainland.

During the summer months, there's a surprising amount of cultural activity, but once the last leaf falls, life gets pretty quiet. Even

151

at the height of the season, there are few shops and limited fine dining. Come winter, the library and schoolhouse are the centers of activity, although plans are in the works to build a new island community center.

As one might imagine, health care on a small island is limited. "Islesboro is not the place to come if you are sick," says an islander who works at the town's health care center. "We have three full-time physician's assistants, and we do the best we can, but it's very hard for residents. For elderly year-rounders, the lack of health care can be horrible. There are few home health care providers here, and no long-term care choices. They end up going into a nursing home on the mainland, and it breaks everyone's heart."

Without a doubt, island living can be inconvenient at times. Nonetheless, despite being tied to the ferry schedule, residents believe the benefits far outweigh the disadvantages. "Islesboro is truly gorgeous," says one retiree. "There are sweeping vistas everywhere. Winding roads end at hidden coves where you can spot seals basking in the sun. It's not only a refuge, but a wonderful year-round community."

⚑ WEATHER

Average Temperature (degrees Fahrenheit): January, 20.9; April, 42.7; July, 68.2; October, 48.4. **Average Annual Rainfall:** 33 inches. **Average Annual Snowfall:** 61.3 inches.

⚑ TAXES

Property Tax Rate: $11.99 per $1,000 valuation. **Ratio to Current Market Value:** 80%.

⚑ REAL ESTATE

Provided by Don Pendleton, Islesboro Realty (207-734-6488)
Older Housing Stock: "Fixer-uppers" do not exist. **Good Condition:**

A typical older home on beautiful Islesboro. PHOTO BY DON PENDLETON

$195,000 to $395,000 with no water view. **Waterfront Locations**: $450,000 and up. **Buildable Lots**: $65,000 to $125,000. **Waterfront Lots**: $200,000 to $750,000.

⚓ RETIREMENT LIVING

Islesboro has no retirement communities.

⚓ PUBLIC SAFETY

Crimes per 1,000 Population for Waldo County, 2000: 8.48. **Non-emergency Police**: 207-734-6787. **Non-emergency Fire**: 207-734-6787. **Emergency**: 911.

Leslie Radcliffe, Islesboro's public safety officer, says, "Although we do have part-time law enforcement, there's not really any crime to speak of. Islesboro is a very safe, quiet little community."

⚓ HEALTH CARE

Closest Hospitals: Waldo County General Hospital (207-338-2500, www.wchi.com) in Belfast is an acute-care facility offering a full range of diagnostic, therapeutic, and health education services. Penobscot Bay Medical Center (207-596-8000) in Rockport offers a twenty-four-hour emergency room along with comprehensive medical, surgical, psychiatric, cardiac, and cancer care. **Home Health Care**: Kno-Wal-Lin Home Health Care (207-594-9561). **Clinics**: Islesboro Health Center (207-734-2213) has twenty-four-hour emergency care.

♣ CONTINUING EDUCATION

Senior College: University of Maine, Hutchinson Center (207-338-8002; www.hutchinsoncenter.umain.edu/seniorcollege.html) in Belfast. **Colleges and Universities**: University of Maine, Hutchinson Center (207-338-8002; www.hutchinsoncenter.umain.edu/seniorcollege.html) in Belfast. **Adult Education Programs**: Islesboro Central School (207-734-6723).

♣ LIBRARY

207-734-2218

♣ HISTORICAL SOCIETY

207-734-6733

♣ SPECIFICALLY FOR SENIORS

The Islesboro Health Center (207-734-2213) sponsors special programs for seniors. The library (207-734-2218) has community-wide programs as well.

♣ VOLUNTEERING

The Islesboro Islands Trust (207-734-6907) and the Islesboro Historical Society (207-734-6733) welcome volunteers.

♣ RECREATION

Golf: The Tarratine Club (207-734-2248) is a private course. **Tennis Courts**: By the soccer field in the middle of the island; also at the Tarratine Club. **Parks**: Pendleton Point Town Beach has picnic tables; Sprague's Beach is lovely for beachcombing. **Running/Walking/Biking**: Biking around the island is popular with tourists and residents. **Fitness Classes**: The Islesboro Health Center (207-734-2213) sponsors a few classes; the Penobscot Bay YMCA (207-236-3375) in Rockport is also popular with islanders. **Hunting/Fishing**: Call the Town Office for licenses at 207-734-2253. **Skiing**: Residents cross-country ski on the golf course; closest downhill ski area is the Camden Snow Bowl (207-236-3438).

Alice L. Pendleton Library
P.O. Box 77
309 Main Road, Islesboro

Hours:
Monday and Wednesday, 10:00 a.m. to 12:00 noon; 1:30 to 4:30 p.m.
Saturday and Sunday, 1:30 to 4:30 p.m.

Alice L. Pendleton Library was a product of the enthusiasm and hard work of the late Alice Lavinia Pendleton, known affectionately as Miss Alice, of Islesboro and Brooklyn, New York. The granite-and-brick structure houses a collection of more than 20,000 items, with a small computer network and several workstations. In addition to book discussion groups, children's programs, and special events, the library has Internet and e-mail access. For more information about programs, see www.alpl.lib.me.us.

♠ ENTERTAINMENT

Cinemas: None on the island. Closest are in Belfast and Camden.
Museums: Sailor's Memorial Museum. **Theaters**: Islesboro Performing Arts holds programs at the Free Will Baptist Church.

♠ NATURE

Contact the Islesboro Islands Trust (207-734-6907) for a list of conservation sites on the island. Warren Island, a quick kayak trip from the ferry terminal, is a state park with nature trails and picnic tables.

♠ SHOPPING

Two small grocery stores are the mainstays of the island. The Island Market (207-734-6672) offers all kinds of specialty foods and even caters. Durkee's General Store is a full-service store with lunch counter, deli, and gas (207-734-2201). A few small specialty stores are open seasonally.

♠ WHO LIVES HERE

Population: 603. **Median Age**: 45.9. **Percentage Age 62 and Older**: 24.0%. **Percentage with Bachelor's Degree**: 22.5%. **Percentage**

ISLAND LIVING
Could you retire to an island? In all, there are said to be more than 3,000 off the coast of Maine, some of them no bigger than a schooner, with several—Chebeague and Peaks in Casco Bay, and Monhegan, Vinalhaven, North Haven, Matinicus, Isle au Haut, Islesford, and Islesboro in Penobscot Bay—inhabited year-round. The mystique of island living adds another dimension to the Maine retirement experience, and for some, the lure of these special places proves irresistible.

with Graduate or Professional Degree: 12%. Median Household Income: $39,643. Mean Retirement Income: $24,057. Per Capita Income: $ 25,653.

⚑ ESSENTIAL PHONE NUMBERS AND WEB SITES

Chamber of Commerce: Camden–Rockport–Lincolnville Chamber (207-236-4404; www.camdenme.org). **Town Office**: 207-734-2253. **Voter and Vehicle Registration**: Town Clerk's Department (207-734-2253). **Drivers' Licenses**: Motor Vehicle Office in Rockland (207-596-2255).

⚑ LOCAL NEWS

Newspapers: *Islesboro Island News* (207-734-6921). **Community Cable Station**: There is no cable on the island.

⚑ TRANSPORTATION

Bus: Concord Trailways (800-639-3317; www.concordtrailways.com) from Camden. **Closest Airport**: Knox County Airport in Owls Head. **Ferry**: The *Margaret Chase Smith* provides year-round service to Islesboro from nearby Lincolnville Beach (207-789-5611). **Water Taxi**: The *Quicksilver* (207-734-8379) runs between Islesboro and Lincolnville Beach on Thursday and Saturday evenings. **Train**: Amtrak's Downeaster, in Portland. **Traffic**: Light, except at the ferry terminal in season.

⚑ DISTANCE TO OTHER CITIES

Portland, Me. 90.3 miles
Bangor, Me. 51 miles
Boston, Mass. 203.6 miles
New York, N.Y. 403.5 miles
Montreal, Quebec 296.7 miles
Quebec City, Quebec 245.9 miles

♠ JOBS

Islesboro is one of eighteen communities in the Belfast Labor Market. Annual figures for the area in 2001 were: **Civilian Labor Force:** 18,460; **Employed:** 17,760; **Unemployed:** 700; **Unemployment Rate:** 3.3%.

♠ UTILITIES

Electricity: Central Maine Power (800-750-4000). **Water:** Private wells. **Telephone:** Verizon (800-585-4466). **Cable TV:** Adelphia (800-336-9988). **Internet Service Providers:** Midcoast Internet Solutions (207-594-8277; www.midcoast.com).

> *People who retire to Islesboro aren't snowbirds who leave for the winter. Oh, they may go away for a week or two, but they're here year-round because they love it. It's a very special place.*
>
> —Don Pendleton, Islesboro Realty

♠ PLACES OF WORSHIP

There are several churches on the island, including the Free Will Baptist Church, site of the Islesboro Performing Arts series in summer.

♠ EVENTS AND FESTIVALS

The island's two grocery stores are good sources of information for current events, as is the town library.

♠ RESTAURANTS

Year-round dining is limited to sandwiches and subs from the grocery store. In summer, the Dark Harbor House (207-734-6669; www.darkharborhouse.com) offers fine dining by reservation.

♠ LODGING

One of the few places to stay on Islesboro is the Dark Harbor House (207-734-6669; www.darkharborhouse.com). Built in 1896 for a Philadelphia banker, the inn is a striking example of the summer mansions erected along the Maine coast at the turn of the century. A masterpiece of Georgian Revival architecture, it is listed on the National Register of Historic Places. Two bed-and-breakfasts also accommodate guests: Aunt Laura's B & B and Dark Harbor B & B.

⚑ WHAT THE LOCALS SAY

Bob and Marcie Congdon vacationed on Islesboro for forty years before taking the plunge and becoming year-round islanders. "The people and the environment were what drew us here," says Bob. "We were familiar with the community and owned a cabin here. We built a new post-and-beam house and settled into island life."

The Congdons quickly became part of the town's civic fabric, joining boards and volunteering for various committees. They dis-

covered that the island's busy social schedule didn't end with the departure of the summer folk. "There are all kinds of get-togethers in people's homes,"

The Dark Harbor House is a landmark Islesboro business.
PHOTO BY BEN MAGRO

says Bob. He says that the off-season is a special time on Islesboro. "We like the winter here. But we do enjoy getting away during February and March."

When asked how difficult it is to live by a ferry schedule, Bob Congdon shrugs off any inconvenience. "It's something you get used to. In the winter, there aren't as many ferries going back and forth, but there are also no lines. We frequently go to Camden or Rockland to the movies on Thursday nights. We take the ferry over and catch the water taxi on the way back. That taxi has been a real godsend."

One concern for some retirees living on Islesboro is the limited range of health care options. "Fortunately, we have a terrific ambulance service," says Bob Congdon, who has firsthand experience with the community's knowledgeable emergency medical technicians. "A few years ago, I had heart trouble in the middle of the night, and the crew was here within ten minutes. Two hours later, I was in the emergency room at Penobscot Bay Medical Center." And within days, he was back with his wife enjoying the tranquility of his island home.

Grindle Point Light is a beacon for mariners. PHOTO BY TED PANAYOTOFF

Belfast

Waldo County

At a Glance

Land Area: 34.04 square miles
Persons per Square Mile: 187
Population: 6,381
Median Age: 43.3 years
Neighboring Communities: Searsport, Northport, Islesboro, Camden

"Funky" and "artsy" are two adjectives often used to describe the city of Belfast, located on the coast of the upper western portion of Penobscot Bay. Where else can you stroll a downtown street and pass bustling shops offering everything from composting toilets to camouflage clothing, or postcards to pastries? An eclectic array of lifestyles typifies this city of 6,000 or so, lending it a vibrancy usually reserved for much larger urban centers.

One look at the stately eighteenth-century homes lining the city's wide streets, and images of wealthy sea captains and tall-masted schooners come to mind. Indeed, Belfast, along with neighboring Searsport, was once a major center of shipbuilding and shipping. In Belfast, the decline of these maritime industries led to an era of manufacturing. Thanks to two huge poultry processing plants that flourished beginning in the 1940s, the city became known as the world's "Broiler Capital." Forty years or so later, this industry, along with others, flew the coop, and Belfast's economic prospects turned bleak. The 1990s saw the start of an incredible economic rebirth, when MBNA, the world's largest independent credit card lender, moved into Maine, building call centers in several midcoast towns, including a giant complex on the outskirts of Belfast. Almost overnight, impoverished Waldo County became one of the state's fastest growing areas, and Belfast began to blossom.

"Belfast is experiencing many positive changes," says Patti Ann Lord, a local real estate broker. "We've just completed a $12 million expansion at Waldo County Hospital. Our waterfront has undergone substantial improvements, including a lovely walkway along the ocean and a park. The University of Maine opened a campus in town, called the Hutchinson Center, along with a senior college offering a variety of courses. The YMCA has a new building, and the library was just renovated. We are in the midst of a cultural and educational revival, and it's an exciting time."

Despite the changes, Belfast remains a little rough around the edges. It has a refreshingly real, un-touristy feeling, even at the height of summer. The harbor, with the Passagassawakeag River at its head, feels hardworking, despite the many pleasure yachts at their moorings. Stores lining the downtown streets delight visitors "from away," and yet continue to sell useful household items.

"It's a quirky place," says Mike Silverton, who retired here in 2002. "And for us, that's part of Belfast's charm."

⚑ WEATHER
Average Temperature (degrees Fahrenheit): January, 20.9; April, 42.7; July, 68.2; October, 48.4. **Average Annual Rainfall**: 33 inches. **Average Annual Snowfall**: 61.3 inches.

⚑ TAXES
Property Tax Rate: $22 per $1,000 valuation. **Ratio to Current Market Value**: 71%.

⚑ REAL ESTATE
Provided by Patti Ann Lord, Jaret & Cohn Real Estate (207-338-4220)
Older Housing Stock: $125,000 to $500,000, depending on location. **New Custom Construction**: $200,000 to $350,000 and up, depending on size and location. **Waterfront Locations**: $550,000 to

Penobscot Shores offers sweeping views of the ocean. PHOTO BY PAULA JOHNDRO

$1,100,000. **Rental Apartments**: Furnished, $500/week vacation (furnished); $550 to $900/month.

⚐ RETIREMENT LIVING

Penobscot Shores (207-338-2332; www.penobscotshores.com) offers independently owned apartments or cottages. Harbor Hill (207-338-5307) rents units to eighty-two residents.

⚐ PUBLIC SAFETY

Crimes per 1,000 Population, 2000: 29.14. **Non-emergency Police**: 207-338-2420; www.belfastmepd.org. **Non-emergency Fire**: 207-338-3362. **Emergency**: 911.

Allen Weaver, Belfast's chief of police, describes his town as "a quaint coastal community. As one of the fastest growing communities in Waldo County, we have seen our share of the changes that go with economic growth. However, Belfast is still a great—and safe—place to live."

♠ HEALTH CARE

Closest Hospitals: Waldo County General Hospital (207-338-2500, www.wchi.com), located right in Belfast, is an acute-care facility offering a full range of diagnostic, therapeutic, and health education services. **Home Health Care**: Kno-Wal-Lin Home Health Care (207-594-9561). **Long-Term Care Facilities**: Harbor Hill (207-338-5307) provides assisted living, specialized Alzheimer's care, and respite care. Tallpines Health Care Facilities (207-338-4117) offers nursing care.

♠ CONTINUING EDUCATION

Senior College: University of Maine, Hutchinson Center (207-338-8002; www.hutchinsoncenter.umain.edu/seniorcollege.html). **Colleges and Universities**: University of Maine, Hutchinson Center (207-338-8002; www.hutchinsoncenter.umain.edu/seniorcollege.html). **Adult Education Programs**: Belfast Area High School (207-338-3197).

In addition to all that Belfast has to offer, we are less than an hour from Bangor, a city of 30,000 people, and its international airport, greater shopping opportunities, and sophisticated hospital facilities.

—Patti Ann Lord,
Jaret & Cohn Real Estate

♠ LIBRARY

The Belfast Free Library, located at 106 High Street, dates back to 1888 but was completely renovated in 2000 through a building campaign that raised more than $2.6 million (207-338-3884; www.belfastlibrary.org).

♠ HISTORICAL SOCIETY

Belfast Historical Society (207-338-2564).

Located in Belfast, the Hutchinson Center of the University of Maine is named after Frederick E. Hutchinson, who was president of the University of Maine from 1992 to 1997. Using on-site resources and state-of-the-art distance learning technology, the Center provides undergraduate, graduate, and noncredit courses and programs.

↟ SPECIFICALLY FOR SENIORS

The Waldo County YMCA has programs reserved just for seniors (207-338-4598).

↟ VOLUNTEERING

Waldo County General Hospital Aid is an active volunteer group that welcomes new members. Among other activities, Hospital Aid sponsors an annual Silver Tea and Garden Walk (207-548-0266).

↟ RECREATION

Golf: Northport Golf Club is a nine-hole public course (207-338-2270). Searsport Pines is a nine-hole course set among 100-year-old

Belfast Free Library
106 High Street, Belfast

Monday, 9:30 a.m. to 8:00 p.m.
Tuesday, Thursday, and Friday, 9:30 a.m. to 6:00 p.m.
Wednesday, 12:00 noon to 8:00 p.m.
Saturday, 10:00 a.m. to 2:00 p.m.

Belfast Free Library reopened in June 2000 after undergoing a construction project that lasted nearly eighteen months. Now with more than double the useable space, the facility offers expanded programs and services in all departments. On each floor are Internet-ready public computers, and on the third floor is a special collections section. Services include interlibrary loan and Talking Books. Browse www.belfastlibrary.org to learn more.

pines (207-548-2854). **Tennis Courts**: Belfast City Park. **Parks**: Belfast City Park offers an outdoor swimming pool, picnic tables, and a playground, all overlooking the bay. Downtown, Heritage Park provides a great place to watch kayakers and fishermen in the harbor. **Running/Walking/Biking**: Paths at Belfast's two parks as well as the walking track at the YMCA. **Fitness Classes**: Waldo County YMCA, a new, state-of-the-art facility (207-338-4598). **Hunting/Fishing**: Call the city clerk for licenses at 207-338-3370. **Skiing**: Swan Lake in Swanville (eight miles away) is a popular cross-country skiing spot; the closest downhill ski area is the Camden Snow Bowl (207-236-3438).

♣ ENTERTAINMENT

Cinemas: The Colonial Theatre (207-338-1930; www.colonialtheatre.com). **Museums**: Penobscot Marine Museum (207-548-2529; www.penobscotmarinemuseum.org), Belfast Historical Museum

(207-338-2564). **Theaters:** The Belfast Maskers (207-338-9668; www.belfastmaskers.com).

▲ NATURE

Moose Point State Park in Searsport is open from Memorial Day until the end of September and features hiking trails, tidal pools, and an evergreen grove for exploring (207-548-2882).

▲ SHOPPING

Supermarkets are located downtown as well as by the junction of Routes 1 and 3. The nearest mall is in Bangor, thirty-four miles away. A great mix of small specialty stores is located downtown, including Chase's Daily, a bakery; the Belfast Co-Op, a natural foods grocery store; and Colburn Shoe Store, the oldest shoe store in America.

▲ WHO LIVES HERE

Population: 6,381. **Median Age:** 43.3. **Percentage Age 62 and Older:** 23%. **Percentage with Bachelor's Degree:** 18.4%. **Percentage with Graduate or Professional Degree:** 10.7%. **Median Household Income:** $32,400. **Mean Retirement Income:** $17,859. **Per capita Income:** $19,276.

▲ ESSENTIAL PHONE NUMBERS AND WEB SITES

Chamber of Commerce: 207-338-5900, www.belfastmaine.org. **City Hall:** 207-338-3370; www.cityofbelfast.org. **Voter and Vehicle Registration:** City Clerk's Department (207-338-3370, ext. 14). **Drivers' Licenses:** Motor Vehicle Office in Rockland (207-596-2255).

▲ LOCAL NEWS

Newspapers: *The Republican Journal* (207-338-3333), *The Waldo Independent* (207-338-5100). **Community Cable Station:** Channel 7.

Where to Retire in Maine

Community Internet Sites: www.villagesoup.com (207-338-0484), www.belfastmaine.org, www.cityofbelfast.org.

♠ TRANSPORTATION

Bus: Waldo County Transportation (207-338-4769) serves seniors. Concord Trailways (800-639-3317; www.concordtrailways.com) provides daily service from Belfast to Boston. **Ferry**: The *Margaret Chase Smith* provides year-round service to Islesboro from nearby Lincolnville Beach (207-789-5611). **Closest Airport**: Bangor International Airport is thirty-seven miles away. Belfast Municipal Airport provides helicopter service and charters. **Limo Service**: Midcoast Limo (207-236-2424), Superior Limousine (800-340-1155). **Taxi**: Belfast Taxi (207-338-2943). **Traffic**: Usually light; moderate in season.

♠ DISTANCE TO OTHER CITIES

Portland, Me. 97.5 miles

Bangor, Me. 34 miles

Boston, Mass. 208.8 miles

New York, N.Y. 413.7 miles

Montreal, Quebec 282.5 miles

Quebec City, Quebec 231.3 miles

♠ JOBS

Belfast is one of eighteen communities in the Belfast Labor Market. Annual figures for the area in 2001 were: **Civilian Labor Force**: 18,460; **Employed**: 17,760; **Unemployed**: 700; **Unemployment Rate**: 3.3%.

♠ UTILITIES

Electricity: Central Maine Power (800-750-4000). **Water**: Belfast Water District (207-338-1200). **Telephone**: Verizon (800-585-4466).

Cable TV: Adelphia (800-336-9988). **Internet Service Providers**: Midcoast Internet Solutions (207-594-8277).

⚑ PLACES OF WORSHIP
Many of the mainline Protestant as well as Episcopal, Pentecostal, Unitarian-Universalist, and Catholic churches are represented in Belfast. The closest synagogue is Adas Yoshuron in Rockland (207-594-4523).

⚑ EVENTS AND FESTIVALS
Numerous festivals take place throughout the year, including the annual Arts in the Park Festival, held in July; Belfast Bearfest, a summer-long event featuring more than forty fiberglass bears decorated by Maine artists and placed throughout town; and New Year's by the Bay, held in January.

⚑ RESTAURANTS
Dining choices vary from great seafood to rustic fare to ethnic offerings. Try Twilight Café (207-338-0937), Darby's (207-338-2339), Chase's Daily, and Dos Amigos (207-338-3775).

⚑ LODGING
Inns, bed-and-breakfast houses, and motels offer hospitality in the Belfast area. A few suggestions are: The Jeweled Turret Inn (207-338-2304, www.jeweledturret.com), Londonderry Inn (207-338-2763, www.londonderry-inn.com), and Belfast Harbor Inn (207-338-2740, www.belfastharborinn.com).

⚑ WHAT THE LOCALS SAY
Connie and Dana Barnes were one of the first couples to move into Penobscot Shores, a retirement community built in 1996 on twenty

oceanfront acres in Belfast. "We knew we wanted to retire in Maine," says Connie, "and had settled farther up the coast in Searsport. When this community opened, we took one look at the view and moved right in." The Barneses enjoy a convenient lifestyle that includes trips to hear the Bangor Symphony, gourmet meals in the Penobscot Shores dining room, and quiet times at home with their pet cat.

Neighbors Ruth and Richard Goodwin looked at four different retirement communities before settling in Belfast in 2002. "This place felt like home," says Richard, who is originally from York. "We know everybody, and we're only three minutes away from great health care at Waldo County General Hospital."

Mike and Lee Silverton retired to Belfast in 2002, purchasing an 1842 Greek Revival home in Belfast's historic district. "We chose Belfast for its charm and character," says Mike, a former secondary-school English teacher. "We love Chase's and the Co-Op, and the Spring Street Café is a dandy little restaurant."

The Silvertons are self-proclaimed "city people" who wondered whether they'd "make the transition to Maine gracefully." Although delighted with their new home, they offer sage advice for those considering retirement in the Pine Tree State: "Be fond of long, cold winters."

▲▲▲

Central Maine

Kennebec and Androscoggin Counties make up the region known as central Maine. Kennebec, named for the river that passes through Maine's capital city, Augusta, is home to scores of lakes and ponds, including the Forks, one of Maine's major whitewater rafting centers. The south-central county of Androscoggin is also named for a river: the state's third largest, once so toxic it was barely navigable but now, thanks to stringent cleanup measures, a prime spot for kayak and canoe enthusiasts.

Profiled in this section is the Kennebec County town of Belgrade, known for its beautiful chain of lakes and proud, involved citizens. Not far from Belgrade are the cities of Augusta, a growing commercial as well as government center, and Waterville, site of historic Colby College, one of the country's top private liberal arts institutions.

Bucolic Greene, a quiet town on the outskirts of Lewiston and Auburn, is the Androscoggin County town described on the following pages. Greene as well as surrounding towns such as Leeds and Turner offer affordable property in a rural setting only minutes from the bustling centers of commerce and culture known as "L–A." While together the twin cities rival Portland in terms of population, both Lewiston and Auburn are ringed with sleepy towns offering a yesterday kind of small-town charm.

Belgrade

At a Glance

Land Area: 43.25 square miles
Persons per Square Mile: 68.8
Population: 2,978
Median Age: 39.5 years
Neighboring Communities: Augusta, Manchester, Mount Vernon, Oakland

Water is the heart and soul of Belgrade, specifically, water in the form of five pristine lakes: Long Pond, Great Pond, Messalonskee Lake, Salmon Lake, and North Pond. These bodies of water form the town's identity and are the foundation of its economy. Protecting them is of utmost importance; enjoying them is a close second. A favorite summer haven for centuries and the inspiration for the film classic *On Golden Pond*, Belgrade is a destination for all lake lovers. Its population nearly doubles when nonresidents arrive to spend the summer months at their cottages.

"The Belgrades" encompass several neighborhoods, all part of the town of Belgrade: Belgrade Lakes Village, the town's center, as well as North Belgrade and Belgrade Depot. It's a "bedroom community," with employment in town limited to two lumber companies and a manufacturer of concrete products. Small businesses such as restaurants and country stores provide a few year-round jobs, with rental cottages, boys' and girls' camps, marinas, and a golf course adding part-time positions in the summer. The town is located just a few miles northwest of Maine's capital city, Augusta. Nearly as close is the college town of Waterville. Proximity to these two areas means that cultural activities, such as museums, art, music, and drama—if not found in Belgrade—are not far away.

*An angler pulls
out a keeper.*
PHOTO BY JAN PARTRIDGE

Much of Belgrade's acreage
is composed of
lakes, streams,
and wetlands.
Its five lakes
and their inlet/
outlet streams
offer several
species of fish
for those who
enjoy fishing,
plenty of water
surface for boaters, and excellent opportunities for birdwatchers.
In addition to activities on the water, there is a new eighteen-hole
golf course, just south of Belgrade Lakes Village, ranked fifth "Best
New Upscale Public Course in America" by *Golf Digest*, December
1999. Other activities enjoyed by retirees include outdoor concerts
at New England Music Camp on Messalonskee Lake and cultural
and campus events in nearby Waterville, Augusta, Farmington, and
Skowhegan.

Civic pride is high, and residents are especially pleased with
their new community center and its myriad activities, stone fireplace,
covered porch, and spectacular views to the lake. "The Belgrade
Community Center for All Seasons is such an asset to our community," says Tammy Holman of Long Pond Realty. "It truly is a 'center'
in every sense of the word."

⬆ WEATHER

Average Temperature (degrees Fahrenheit): January, 19.5; April, 43.7; July, 70.1; October, 48.8. **Average Annual Rainfall:** 41.67 inches. **Average Annual Snowfall:** 79 inches.

⬆ TAXES

Property Tax Rate: $16.10 per $1,000 valuation. **Ratio to Current Market Value:** 97.5%.

⬆ REAL ESTATE

Provided by Tammy Holman, Long Pond Realty (207-495-9220)
Older Housing Stock: $115,000 to $250,000 depending on location. **New Custom Construction:** $200,000 and up, depending on size and location. **Waterfront Locations:** $300,000 to $1 million. **Rental Apartments:** $400/month.

⬆ RETIREMENT LIVING

The Little Village is a community of modular homes in Belgrade, offering independent living with services (207-495-9229). Granite Hill Estates in Hallowell (207-626-7786; www.granitehillestates.com) offers apartments, cottages, and assisted-living units.

⬆ PUBLIC SAFETY

Crimes per 1,000 Population for Kennebec County, 2000: 23.72. **Non-emergency Police:** Kennebec Sheriff's Department (800-498-1930). **Non-emergency Fire:** 207-465-2555. **Emergency:** 911.

Captain George Madden of the Kennebec Sheriff's Department says, "Belgrade is a tranquil community located in a secure, rural setting. Our department makes only a handful of calls out there, answering minor complaints. It's a peaceful place where many of the state's law enforcement professionals have chosen to live."

♠ HEALTH CARE

Closest Hospitals: Maine General Medical Center has campuses in Waterville and Augusta (207-626-1000; www.MaineGeneral.org). **Clinics**: Belgrade Regional Health Center (207-495-3323). **Long-Term Care Facilities**: Home Choice Health Care (207-495-2115).

♠ CONTINUING EDUCATION

Senior College: Augusta Senior College, University of Maine at Augusta (207-621-3551). **Colleges and Universities**: Closest is University of Maine at Augusta (207-621-3551). **Adult Education Programs**: Messalonskee High School (207-465-7381).

♠ LIBRARY

Belgrade Public Library (207-465-7924).

> *Belgrade is a fantastic community that has something for everyone.*
>
> —Tammy Holman, Long Pond Realty

♠ HISTORICAL SOCIETY

The Belgrade Historical Society is a fledgling group looking for interested members. Call (207-495-9220) to volunteer. History buffs will appreciate this portion of the town's Web site: www.belgrademaine.com/history/history.html.

♠ SPECIFICALLY FOR SENIORS

Union Church of Belgrade Lakes (207-495-3599) offers activities for seniors; the Belgrade Community Center for All Seasons (207-495-3481) has special senior programs.

♠ VOLUNTEERING

Belgrade Recreation Association provides and maintains recreational programs for Belgrade area youth (207-495-2696). Belgrade Historical Society welcomes new members (207-495-9220).

Belgrade Public Library
Belgrade Community Center for All Seasons
Route 27, Belgrade

Hours:
Tuesday, 12:00 noon to 7:00 p.m.
Thursday, 10:00 a.m. to 7:00 p.m.

Housed in the town's new community center, Belgrade Public Library offers interlibrary loan, reader's advisory, reference services, large-print books, and books for children and adults—3,600 volumes in all. The library also features a public-access computer station for Internet research.

⚐ RECREATION

Golf: Belgrade Lakes Golf Club (207-495-4653; www.belgradelakesgolf.com). **Tennis Courts**: Belgrade Central School. **Parks**: Hayden Park, Peninsula Park. **Fitness Classes**: The Belgrade Community Center for All Seasons, located on Route 27 just southwest of Belgrade Lakes Village, is a beautiful new center built in 2000; it offers basketball, volleyball, yoga, and other programs (207-495-3481). **Hunting/Fishing**: Call the Town Office for licenses at 207-495-2258. **Skiing**: The area's frozen, snow-covered lakes are popular with cross-country skiers; closest downhill ski area is Titcomb Mountain (207-778-9031; www.titcombmountain.com).

⚐ ENTERTAINMENT

Cinemas: Hoyt's Cinema in Augusta is ten minutes away. **Museums**: Maine State Museum in Augusta. **Theaters**: New England Music Camp on Messalonskee Lake.

♠ NATURE

Scenic French's Mountain and Blueberry Hill offer spectacular views of the lakes. Both trails start from Watson Pond Road, off Route 27.

♠ SHOPPING

Supermarkets are located right in Belgrade. The nearest mall is in Auburn. A number of small specialty stores, such as Balloons & Things (207-495-3864), Christy's Country Store (207-495-8861), The Enchanted Swan (207-495-2264), and Day's Store (207-495-2205), are located in town.

♠ WHO LIVES HERE

Population: 2,978. **Median Age**: 39.5. **Percentage Age 62 and Older**: 14.7%. **Percentage with Bachelor's Degree**: 14.8%.

The first hole of the Belgrade Lakes Golf Club overlooks Great Pond.
PHOTO BY NATE FULLING

177

Percentage with Graduate or Professional Degree: 7.0%. Median Household Income: $39,053. Mean Retirement Income: $13,944. Per Capita Income: $20,407.

⚑ ESSENTIAL PHONE NUMBERS AND WEB SITES

Chamber of Commerce: Belgrade Lakes Region (888-895-2744; www.BelgradeLakesMaine.com). Town Office: 207-495-2258; www.belgrademaine.com. Voter and Vehicle Registration: Town Clerk's Department (207-495-2258). Drivers' Licenses: Motor Vehicle Office in Augusta (207-287-3330).

⚑ LOCAL NEWS

Community Cable Station: Channel 9. Community Internet Sites: www.belgrademaine.com.

⚑ TRANSPORTATION

Tours: The mailboat tour around Long Lake is very popular in the summer. Closest Airport: Augusta Airport. Traffic: Usually light; moderate in season.

⚑ DISTANCE TO OTHER CITIES

Portland, Me. 62.5 miles
Bangor, Me. 69.1 miles
Boston, Mass. 173.9 miles
New York, N.Y. 378.7 miles
Montreal, Quebec 244.8 miles
Quebec City, Quebec 205.9 miles

⚑ JOBS

Belgrade is one of twenty-nine communities in the Augusta Labor Market. Annual figures for the area in 2001 were: Civilian Labor

Force: 46,850; Employed: 44,940; Unemployed: 1,910; Unemployment Rate: 4.1%.

♠ UTILITIES

Electricity: Central Maine Power (800-750-4000). Water: Private wells. Telephone: Verizon (800-585-4466). Cable TV: Adelphia (800-336-9988). Internet Service Providers: A2Z Computing Services (207-872-5981).

♠ PLACES OF WORSHIP

There are half a dozen churches in Belgrade, including the North Belgrade Baptist Church and St. Mark's Episcopal. The closest synagogue, Temple Beth El, is located in Augusta.

♠ EVENTS AND FESTIVALS

Numerous festivals take place throughout the year, including an art festival in July, a Loon Festival in August, Octoberfest in October, and The Christmas Stroll at the beginning of December.

♠ RESTAURANTS

There are only three restaurants in Belgrade, so reservations are strongly suggested. The Sunset Grille (207-495-2439) serves casual fare; the Village Inn (207-495-3553; www.villageinnducks.com) offers waterside dining; and Wings Hill Inn (207-495-2400; www.wingshillinn.com) has, in the words of a local innkeeper, "exquisite food." The Thai Star (207-621-2808) is between Belgrade and Augusta and features superb fresh seafood dishes.

♠ LODGING

Talbot's Bed & Breakfast (207-495-2868) faces the golf course and serves home-cooked breakfasts. Yeaton Farm Inn (207-495-3841;

www.yeatonfarminn.com) is a historic farmhouse with five bedrooms and was once an 1826 stagecoach stop. Wings Hill Inn (207-495-2400; www.wingshillinn.com) has eight rooms on two acres with lovely views of Long Pond.

▲ WHAT THE LOCALS SAY

Imogene and Sam Casey moved to Belgrade in the 1990s from Pittsburgh, Pennsylvania, to be nearer to their daughter. "We loved it here from the day we moved in," says Imogene. "We'd been told that New Englanders were cold, unfriendly folks and that we wouldn't be accepted, but we found Maine to be completely different. Everyone was very nice, warm and helpful."

Both Imogene and Sam became involved in a small church in Belgrade, and soon they were busier than they'd been before retirement. "Sam was a computer programmer, and he started helping the church office with programs and sermons," Imogene says. "I'd been a music teacher, and although I didn't want to teach, I began helping several music students." When Sam died several years later, Imogene's relatives back in Pennsylvania automatically assumed she'd return to her earlier home. "I told them no, that I'd found Maine, and that I wasn't going to leave it.

"I go down there to visit," she says, "but I miss the pace here. After three days in Pennsylvania, I'm ready to go home."

Imogene continues to be active in community affairs and has served as president of the Health Center. "I can't say enough good things about our doctors and hospitals. The medical care that I've experienced, and that my husband received, has been excellent.

"Belgrade is a wonderful place," Imogene enthuses. "The people are caring, and it's beautiful every single season. But personally, I think the whole state is gorgeous."

▲▲▲

Greene
Androscoggin County

At a Glance

Land Area: 32.39 square miles
Persons per Square Mile: 125
Population: 4,076
Median Age: 36.9 years
Neighboring Communities: Turner, Wales, Lewiston

Greene, a quiet, rural town named after Major General Nathan Greene of the Continental Army, lies almost exactly in the center of Androscoggin County, the "Heart of Maine." Although Greene was believed to produce the first shingles sawed in Maine, today the town's sawmills no longer operate. Present-day Greene is a sleepy bedroom community for the twin cities of Lewiston and Auburn, which are about fifteen minutes away, as well as Augusta, a half-hour drive down Route 202. Less than an hour from the coast, mountains, and Portland, Greene is a convenient choice for retirees who want to be near it all.

And there's quite a bit to be near. Lewiston and Auburn (known as "L–A") have changed in the past several years, becoming together one of the state's most important economic centers. The two cities also serve as a major transportation hub, offering two turnpike exits (with direct access to I-95 and I-495) and a municipal airport. Much of the rest of Androscoggin County has changed as well, transforming from a textile-and-shoe center to a progressive health care, tourism, and high-precision manufacturing powerhouse. Meanwhile, Greene has remained quietly residential. But for the traffic on Route 202, you'd hardly guess that nearly half of Maine's population lives within a thirty-mile radius.

The hub of Greene is called Greene Village. It's where the town library, Grange Hall, and historical society are located. Recreation Park, located behind Greene Central School, is busy during the warm weather months and offers residents a place to walk along several marked nature trails. While Greene itself has little in the way of night-life (there are only two restaurants in town), those who live here say they can find all the activity they desire just a short drive away. Many mention Bates College in Lewiston as an important cultural draw.

Founded in 1855, Bates is recognized as one of the nation's premier liberal arts institutions. Throughout the year, the college offers more than 100 concerts ranging from classical to folk music, lectures, art exhibits, dance, and theater. There are the popular free Noonday Concerts every Tuesday throughout the school year as well as the nationally renowned Bates Dance Festival. In addition to Bates, Husson College and branches of both the University of Maine at Augusta and the University of Southern Maine contribute to the cultural landscape. L–A offers much in the way of museums, theaters, and shopping—enough to keep any arts lover happy.

Although it is very rural in nature, there is a real sense of community in Greene. People here are often described as "warm" and "caring": apt descriptors for folks living in the middle of the "Heart of Maine."

♣ WEATHER
Average Temperature (degrees Fahrenheit): January, 19.5; April, 43.7; July, 70.1; October, 48.8. **Average Annual Rainfall:** 41.67 inches. **Average Annual Snowfall:** 79.5 inches.

♣ TAXES
Property Tax Rate: $16.40 per $1,000 valuation. **Ratio to Current Market Value:** 105%.

♣ REAL ESTATE
Provided by Mary Ann Norcross, ERA Worden Real Estate (207-784-0159)
Older Housing Stock: $95,000 to $250,000, depending on location.

Seniors at The Meadows enjoy active social lives.

PHOTOS BY DENISE SCAMMON

New Custom Construction: $150,000 and up, depending on size and location. **Lakefront Locations**: $175,000 and up. **Riverfront Lots**: $40,000 and up.

⚓ RETIREMENT LIVING

The Meadows (207-946-3007; www.mainemeadows.com) is a twenty-three-room, home-style, assisted-living center for self-sufficient seniors in Greene. Several other retirement areas are located nearby: Schooner Retirement (207-784-2900; www.schoonerestates.com) and Clover Health Care (207-784-3573; www.mainecare.com) in Auburn, as well as Monticello Heights (207-786-7149) in Lewiston.

⚓ PUBLIC SAFETY

Crimes per 1,000 Population for Androscoggin County, 2000: 35.79. **Non-emergency Police**: 207-784-7361. **Non-emergency Fire**: 207-946-5936. **Emergency**: 911.

Deputy "Mac" MacMillan of the Androscoggin County Sheriff's Department knows the town of Greene well. "We get calls for speeding and minor things in Greene, but by and large, it's a safe and quiet community," he says.

⚑ HEALTH CARE
Closest Hospitals: Central Maine Medical Center (CMMC) is a 250-bed regional referral center offering the most comprehensive range of services of any

> *Greene is an affordable community, located only minutes from Lewiston and yet still in the country.*
>
> —Mary Ann Norcross, ERA Worden Real Estate

hospital in this region (207-795-0111). St. Mary's Regional Medical Center (207-777-8100) is a 233-bed, acute-care medical center that brings the best of medical technology, preventive services, and a "whole person" approach to serving the needs of the region. **Long-Term Care Facilities**: Androscoggin Home Care & Hospice (AHCH) is a nonprofit Medicare-certified agency providing skilled home care, long-term care, and hospice services (207-777-7740).

⚑ CONTINUING EDUCATION
Senior College: Lewiston–Auburn Senior College, University of Southern Maine (207-753-6500). **Colleges and Universities**: Rated among the top twenty-five national liberal arts colleges by *U.S. News & World Report*, Bates College (207-786-6255; www.bates.edu) in nearby Lewiston was founded in 1855 and was the first co-educational college in New England. Husson College (207-786-2114; www.husson.edu) shares 20,000 square feet with the Creative Photographic Art Center of Maine and offers expanded degree programs and facilities. The University of Maine at Augusta at Lewiston–Auburn College is committed to providing convenient access to its students. **Adult Education Programs**: In nearby Turner (207-225-3478).

▲ LIBRARY

Julia Adams Morse Library (207-946-5544).

▲ HISTORICAL SOCIETY

Greene Historical Society, 1092 North River Road, Greene, ME 04236. The Androscoggin Historical Society (207-784-0586) was established in 1923 and maintains the Davis-Wagg Museum and the Clarence March Library.

▲ SPECIFICALLY FOR SENIORS

Greene Senior Citizens Club. Contact Richard Sanford (207-946-5356).

▲ VOLUNTEERING

Your help is welcomed at the Greene Historical Society (1092 North River Road in Greene), at the Julia Adams Morse Library (207-946-5544), and at the White Dove Food Agency (207-946-5838).

Julia Adams Morse Library
105 Main Street, Greene

Hours:
Tuesday, 1:00 to 7:00 p.m.
Thursday, 1:00 to 6:00 p.m.
Saturday, 10:00 a.m. to 3:00 p.m.

Julia Adams Morse Library is an important part of community life in Greene. In 1999, land adjoining the current brick-and-wooden building was purchased for expansion. This project is ongoing with the help of many volunteers. To view pictures of the proposed addition, check out www.townofgreene.net/jamlibrary.

♠ RECREATION

Golf: Springbrook Golf Club (207-946-5900), a challenging eighteen-hole championship course in nearby Leeds, is open to the public. The Turner Highlands Country Club (207-224-7060) has eighteen holes and spectacular views in all directions. **Tennis Courts**: Greene Central School. **Parks**: Recreation Park, behind Greene Central School, has a system of nature trails. Mount Apatite Park (207-784-0191) is a 325-acre wooded park located in the western section of Auburn. **Running/Walking/Biking**: Along the rural roads. **Fitness Classes**: YMCA (207-795-4095) in Auburn, YWCA (207-795-4052) in Lewiston. **Hunting/Fishing**: Call the Town Office for licenses at 207-946-5146. **Skiing**: Cross-country ski trails are behind Greene Central School. Closest downhill ski area is Lost Valley (207-784-1561) in Auburn.

♠ ENTERTAINMENT

Cinemas: Hoyt's Cinema in Auburn, Flagship Cinema in Lewiston. **Museums**: Davis-Wagg Museum (207-784-0586). The Bates College Museum of Art (207-786-6158), located in the Olin Arts Center. **Theaters**: Bates College theater productions (207-786-6161) take place in Schaeffer and Gannett Halls and in the Black Box. Community Little Theatre in Auburn has provided professional-quality, live productions for decades at Great Falls Performing Arts Center in Auburn (207-783-0958). L/A Arts is a community-based local arts agency that presents four performance series: the Mainstage Series, which features live, professional performing arts events in dance and music; the Family Series; the International Film Series; and the Cabaret Series, geared to audiences who are looking for something a bit different (207-782-3200; www.thepublictheatre.org). **Music**: Free Noonday Concerts take place every Tuesday at 12:30 p.m. throughout the school year (excluding school vacations and holi-

days) in the Olin Arts Center Concert Hall (207-786-6135; www
.mainemusicsociety.org).

⚑ NATURE

For a map of Greene's nature trail system, click on the town's Web
site (www.townofgreene.net) and go to "recreational activities."
Thorncrag Bird Sanctuary (207-782-5238), the largest bird sanctuary
in New England, is a 310-acre wildlife preserve located within the
city limits of Lewiston.

⚑ SHOPPING

Greene has few stores; however, there is a grocery store, the Greene
IGA, located on Route 202. The nearest mall is in Portland.

⚑ WHO LIVES HERE

Population: 4,076. **Median Age**: 36.9. **Percentage Age 62 and
Older**: 11%. **Percentage with Bachelor's Degree**: 8.5%. **Percentage
with Graduate or Professional Degree**: 2.7%. **Median Household
Income**: $48,017. **Mean Retirement Income**: $10,026. **Per Capita
Income**: $19,452.

⚑ ESSENTIAL PHONE NUMBERS AND WEB SITES

Chamber of Commerce: Androscoggin County Chamber of Commerce (207-783-2249; www.androscoggincounty.com). **Town Office**:
207-946-5146; www.townofgreene.net. **Voter and Vehicle Registration**: Town Clerk's Department (207-946-5146). **Drivers' Licenses**:
Motor Vehicle Office in Lewiston (207-753-7750).

⚑ LOCAL NEWS

Newspapers: *Sun-Journal/Sunday* (207-784-5411) and *Twin City Times*
(207-795-5017) are both in Lewiston. **Community Cable Station**:

Channel 9. **Community Internet Sites**: www.townofgreene.net, www.androscoggincounty.com.

♠ TRANSPORTATION
Bus: Hudson Bus Lines (207-783-2033) in Lewiston. **Closest Airport**: Auburn–Lewiston Municipal Airport (207-786-0631), Twin Cities Air Service (207-784-6318). **Limo Service**: Supreme Limousine (207-946-7007). **Train**: None, but the U.S. Department of Transportation recently designated the rail lines from Portland to Lewiston a high-speed rail corridor, setting the stage for future passenger rail service from Boston to L–A and Montreal. **Traffic**: Route 202 can be busy.

♠ DISTANCE TO OTHER CITIES
Portland, Me. 44.0 miles
Bangor, Me. 95.7 miles
Boston, Mass. 152.4 miles
New York, N.Y. 357.2 miles
Montreal, Quebec 233.3 miles
Quebec City, Quebec 236.0 miles

♠ JOBS
Greene is one of nine communities in the Lewiston–Auburn Labor Market. Annual figures for the area in 2001 were: **Civilian Labor Force**: 53,700; **Employed**: 51,600; **Unemployed**: 2,100; **Unemployment Rate**: 4.0%.

♠ UTILITIES
Electricity: Central Maine Power (800-750-4000). **Water**: Private wells. **Telephone**: Verizon (800-585-4466). **Cable TV**: Adelphia (800-336-9988). **Internet Service Providers**: Adelphia (800-336-9988).

The dining room of the historic Sedgley Place. PHOTO BY PHIL AND LORRAINE WILBUR

⚑ PLACES OF WORSHIP

Although Greene has only one church, Greene Baptist Church, there are dozens in the surrounding communities.

⚑ EVENTS AND FESTIVALS

Androscoggin is a festival-loving county! There are the Bates Dance Festival, the Maine State Parade, the Liberty Festival, and the beautiful Great Falls Balloon Festival. The Moxie Festival, held in nearby Lisbon Falls every July, honors the distinctive Maine beverage called Moxie, while the Festival de Joie celebrates Lewiston and Auburn's strong and proud Franco-American heritage and culture.

⚑ RESTAURANTS

Greene offers two dining choices: The Sedgley Place (207-946-5990) is a country inn serving five-course dinners, and Mario's of Greene (207-946-5353) serves casual fare. Landry's, a local convenience store, has sandwiches and other fast food and is always busy on Friday and Saturday nights.

⚑ LODGING

There are no places to stay in Green; however, Lewiston and Auburn have many hotels, motels, and B & Bs. Contact the Androscoggin County Chamber of Commerce (207-783-2249; www.androscoggincounty.com) for more information.

⚑ WHAT THE LOCALS SAY

"I lived in Lewiston for forty years before retiring to Greene in 2001," says Charles Peillet. "Greene is a small town, what you might call a bedroom community. I always tell people, 'Don't sneeze as you go through town, or you'll miss it.'"

Charles lives on Sabattus Pond, an area where he'd fished for great northern pike for decades. He feels that Greene has much to offer retirees, mainly because of the caring people that live there. "We have a real opportunity for growth in this town. We're close to Lewiston and Auburn, plus we're on Route 202, which heads to Augusta. Our challenge in Greene is to grow and yet avoid suburban sprawl."

Charles has been involved in town affairs since moving to Greene. "One of the first things I did was to join the Pond Association and the Androscoggin Valley Conservation Commission. It is easy to get involved here, if you are willing."

"I feel so blessed to live here," he says. "I'm looking out my window right now at the sun sparkling on the snow-covered lake, and it is just gorgeous. I've lived on three continents, and sometimes I think we Mainers don't realize exactly what we've got. To me, Maine is like a small Switzerland."

🌲🌲🌲

Northern Maine

The counties of Somerset, Aroostook, Piscataquis, and Penobscot make up the vast region known as northern Maine. The three main industries of this region are logging, tourism, and agriculture. Somerset, with a land area of 3,903 square miles, is Maine's second largest county. Extending from the Canadian border to Fairfield, the area is almost ninety percent forested and borders Moosehead Lake and the Allagash Wilderness Waterway. Flagstaff Lake as well as much of the Dead River, a popular rafting spot, are located in Somerset County, as is Skowhegan, the home of Margaret Chase Smith, the first woman to serve in both the U.S. House and Senate.

Aroostook covers an area larger than Rhode Island and Connecticut combined, and is the state's largest shire. Known simply as "the County," Aroostook contains several communities including the town of Fort Kent, part of the St. John River Valley and home to a branch of the University of Maine. Piscataquis, meaning "rapid waters" in Algonquin, is Maine's third largest county and contains 200,000-acre Baxter State Park as well as Maine's highest mountain, Katahdin. Baxter was a gift to the state by Governor Percival Baxter, who stipulated that the park be kept forever wild for the people of Maine. Piscataquis County also contains much of the Allagash Wilderness Waterway.

Heavily forested, with a low population density, Piscataquis County has about 18,000 residents. The town of Dover-Foxcroft, profiled on pages 203 to 212, is the area's largest community and a business center for the surrounding area. It is situated on the Piscataquis River and boasts lovely old homes and tree-lined streets.

Finally, there is Penobscot County—and a surprising statistic: this county, named for the mighty river that meanders through the region, has the most towns in Maine. Along the river lies the largest city in the region, Bangor. Although it was once known only for its colorful history as a logging town, this city of 31,000 residents now enjoys state-of-the-art health care facilities, a lively arts scene, and increasing importance in foreign trade and travel.

Bangor   *Penobscot County*

At a Glance

Land Area: 34.45 square miles
Persons per Square Mile: 913
Population: 31,473
Median Age: 36.1 years
Neighboring Communities: Orono, Hampden, Hermon, Brewer

Maine's third largest city sits thirty miles up the Penobscot River and is the retail hub for central, eastern, and northern Maine. Described in the 1800s as the "undisputed lumber capital of the world," Bangor has many reminders of its heyday: a thirty-five-foot-tall statue of legendary logger Paul Bunyan on Main Street; a sculpture entitled "The River Drivers" in Peirce Memorial Park on Harlow Street; and several impressive mansions, once owned by the lumber barons, which line the heart of downtown. A stroll along the Broadway Historic District gives a glimpse of those extravagant times, a boom period when the city's mills are said to have shipped more than 246 million board feet of lumber in a year.

Today the downtown of the "Queen City" is making strides to reinvent itself after years of losing businesses to malls and shopping centers. Small shops, restaurants, and galleries have taken up residence in the old brick and granite buildings, and the city is touting gems such as the renovated and expanded Bangor Public Library (whose circulation is one of the highest per capita in New England) as well as the lovely little parks such as Norumbega Parkway and Kenduskeag Mall that bring trees and flowers to the heart of the downtown. Even more exciting for Bangor's future is the thirty-six-acre Penobscot Riverfront Development Project, now underway and slated to bring office buildings, housing, and public access to the riverfront.

Bangor is often described as a convenient place to live. Residents enjoy the proximity of the city to two indoor shopping malls, an international airport, the second largest hospital in the state, and several institutions of higher learning. The University of Maine, with its NCAA Division I athletics program and the state's largest library, is only twelve miles north of the city, in Orono. UMaine also offers

Boats wait in the Penobscot. PHOTO BY TAMMI YOUNGBLOOD OF CUSTOM IMAGING

the Maine Center for the Arts, which attracts dozens of world-class acts in theater, music, and dance each year.

Retirees appreciate the Hammond Street Senior Center, one of the downtown's busiest destinations. "We have 1,800 people registered for our programs," says Mindy Martin, who works at the center. "We not only have classes in things like yoga, line dancing, and pottery, but we sponsor concerts, lunches, and monthly teas." The nonprofit center was started by a couple from Connecticut and supports itself partly through a popular gift shop and a busy thrift store. When they aren't volunteering at the shops, practicing the two-step or working out in the center's gym, Bangor's seniors take day trips to Canada and longer jaunts to Jackman, Maine, where the center owns a lodge. "This place is one of Bangor's best-kept secrets," says Mindy.

There's a fierce loyalty among residents of Bangor. Even author Stephen King, who could live anywhere in the world, chooses to stay in his hometown. Hilma Adams, a local realtor, sums it up this way: "I have been the length of the Eastern Seaboard and out to the West, and I must say that Bangor, Maine, is the most wonderful of all the places that I have been."

▲ WEATHER
Average Temperature (degrees Fahrenheit): January, 18; April, 42.9; July, 69.2; October, 47.8. **Average Annual Rainfall:** 41.05 inches. **Average Annual Snowfall:** 78.2 inches.

▲ TAXES
Property Tax Rate: $23.60 per $1,000 valuation. **Ratio to Current Market Value:** 100%.

▲ REAL ESTATE
Provided by Louise Rolnick, Town & Country Realtors (207-942-6711)
Older Housing Stock: $90,000 to $350,000, depending on location.

New Custom Construction: $250,000 and up, depending on size and location. Waterfront Locations: $300,000. Riverfront Lots: $100,000. Rental Apartments: $650/month.

⬥ RETIREMENT LIVING

Sunbury Village (207-262-9600; www.sunburyvillage.net) has 115 independent-living apartments. Boyd Place (207-941-2837) has independent-living apartments as well as assisted-living options. Park East Retirement Villa (207-947-7992) has sixteen independent-living apartments. Farther afield, Dirigo Pines in Orono (207-866-3400; www.dirigopines.com) offers cottages and apartments with independent- and assisted-living options, and Avalon Village (207-862-5100; www.avalon-maine.com) in Hampden has sixty cottage units and nine independent-living apartments.

⬥ PUBLIC SAFETY

Crimes per 1,000 Population, 2000: 56.87. Non-emergency Police: 207-947-7384. Non-emergency Fire: 207-942-6335. Emergency: 911.

Don Winslow, Bangor's police chief, reports, "The city of Bangor is one of the safest communities in which people may work, reside, or visit. We are very proud that Bangor's violent crime rate is ranked the second safest in the country when compared to metropolitan areas of comparable size, and is 2.4 times less than the average of cities of similar size."

⬥ HEALTH CARE

Closest Hospitals: Eastern Maine Medical Center (207-973-7000; www.emh.org) is the second largest hospital in the state, with 411 beds. The hospital provides twenty-four-hour emergency care, is one of three hospitals in the Maine Trauma Center system, and has a helipad for Maine's LifeFlight air ambulance service. St. Joseph Hospital (207-262-1000) provides 100 beds, a twenty-four-hour emergency room, and a wide range of diagnostic testing, including magnetic resonance imaging. Acadia Hospital (207-973-6100) has 100 acute-care beds for the treatment of mental illness and substance abuse.

♦ CONTINUING EDUCATION

Senior College: Penobscot Valley Senior College, University of Maine Center of Aging, Orono (207-581-1947). **Colleges and Universities**: Bangor Theological Seminary (207-942-6781), Husson College (207-941-7129), University of Maine (207-581-3743; www.umaine.edu). **Adult Education Programs**: Bangor Adult and Community Education (207-945-4400).

♦ LIBRARY

Bangor Public Library (207-947-8336; www.bpl.lib.me.us).

♦ HISTORICAL SOCIETY

Bangor Historical Society (207-942-5766).

♦ SPECIFICALLY FOR SENIORS

Hammond Street Senior Center (207-262-5532) in downtown Bangor has art classes, pottery, yoga, and even trips to the center's own lodge in Jackman, Maine.

♦ VOLUNTEERING

Retirees are welcomed at the Cole-Land Transportation Museum (207-990-3600), at the Hammond Street Senior Center (207-262-5532), at Bangor Public Library (207-947-8336), and at area hospitals.

♦ RECREATION

Golf: Bangor Municipal has twenty-seven championship holes (207-941-0232). Hermon Meadow Golf Course (207-848-3741) is family owned. **Tennis Courts**: Bangor Tennis & Recreation (207-942-4836).

Parks: Bangor has many parks. A few to explore are Broadway Park with its towering trees; Grotto Cascade Park with its twenty-foot-high waterfall overlooking the Penobscot River; and Davenport Park, which features a memorial to the battleship *Maine*. **Running/Walking/Biking**: Prentiss Woods (Grandview Avenue), Brown Woods (Ohio Street), City Forest (Kittredge Road and Tripp Drive), and Essex Woods (Essex Street). Also, UMaine offers walking and bicycle trails. **Fitness Classes**: Bangor YMCA (207-941-2815; www.BangorYMCA .org), Bangor–Brewer YWCA (207-941-2808; www.ywcabb.org), Gold's Gym (207-947-0763). **Hunting/Fishing**: Call City Hall for licenses at 207-945-4400. **Skiing**: Cross-country skiers take advantage of Bangor's many parks as well as the snow-covered terrain of Bangor Municipal Golf Course. Closest downhill ski area is New Hermon Mountain (207-848-5192).

⚡ ENTERTAINMENT

Cinemas: By the mall. **Museums**: Bangor Historical Society Museum (207-942-5766), Cole-Land Transportation Museum (207-990-3600), Hudson Museum at UMaine (207-581-1906), Carnegie Hall Museum of Art in Orono (207-581-3255). **Music**: Bangor Symphony Orchestra (207-942-5555). **Theaters**: Maine Center for the Arts in Orono (207-581-3255). Penobscot Theatre Company (207-942-3333) is Bangor's live, professional theater company.

Tributes to Bangor's past as the "lumber capital of the world" include this handsome monument.
PHOTO BY TAMMI YOUNGBLOOD
OF CUSTOM IMAGING

⚑ NATURE

The Kenduskeag Stream Trail is a two-mile-long wooded path hugging the stream's banks and offering two lookouts. Fields Pond Nature Center in nearby Holden has guided nature trails and exhibits (207-989-2591).

⚑ SHOPPING

Supermarkets are conveniently located around the city. The brick buildings of downtown Bangor have many unique and interesting shops, such as Cadillac Mountain Sports and the Grasshopper Shop. Farther afield, the Bangor Mall on Stillwater Avenue has large anchor stores such as Filene's and JC Penney. The Airport Mall has more than eighty smaller stores.

> *The Bangor region is ideal for retirees because of the medical center, airport, and university, plus we are only an hour from the coast and an hour and a half from the mountains.*
>
> —Louise Rolnick, Town & Country Realtors

⚑ WHO LIVES HERE

Population: 31,473. **Median Age:** 36.1. **Percentage Age 62 and Older:** 16.2%. **Percentage with Bachelor's Degree:** 16.4%. **Percentage with Graduate or Professional Degree:** 10.2%. **Median Household Income:** $29,740. **Mean Retirement Income:** $14,156. **Per Capita Income:** $19,295.

⚑ ESSENTIAL PHONE NUMBERS AND WEB SITES

Chamber of Commerce: 207-947-0307; www.bangorregion.com. **City Hall:** 207-945-4400; www.bgrme.org. **Voter and Vehicle Registration:** City Hall (207-945-4400). **Drivers' Licenses:** Motor Vehicle Office (207-942-1319). **Newcomers Organization:** Bangor–Brewer YWCA (207-941-2808; www.ywcabb.org/new.htm).

♠ LOCAL NEWS

Newspapers: *Bangor Daily News* (207-990-8000; www.bangornews.com) is one of the few remaining family-owned dailies in the country. *Bangor Broadside* (207-262-5800) is published twice a month, while *The Weekly* (207-990-8000) is published (naturally) every week. **Community Cable Station**: Channels 2, 4, and 12. **Community Internet Sites**: www.bangor-info.com.

♠ TRANSPORTATION

Bus: Concord Trailways (800-639-3317; www.concordtrailways.com) provides daily service from Bangor to South Station in Boston, and points between, as well as to northern Maine. Greyhound Lines (800-229-9424) also provides service along U.S. Route 1, with stops from Portland to Bangor. **Tours**: Best of Bangor Bus Tours (207-942-5766). **Closest Airport**: Bangor International Airport. **Taxi**: Bangor–Brewer R & L Taxi (207-942-2225), Harold's Taxi (207-942-8752). **Limo Service**: Black Bear Taxi and Limousine Service (207-827-2288). **Traffic**: Can be busy during rush hours.

♠ DISTANCE TO OTHER CITIES

Portland, Me. 129.1 miles

Boston, Mass. 240.5 miles

New York, N.Y. 445.3 miles

Montreal, Quebec 286.7 miles

Quebec City, Quebec 227.0 miles

♠ JOBS

Bangor is one of fifteen communities in the Bangor Metropolitan Statistical Area. Annual figures for the area in 2001 were: **Civilian Labor Force**: 52,900; **Employed**: 51,000; **Unemployed**: 1,500; **Unemployment Rate**: 2.8%.

▲ UTILITIES

Electricity: Bangor Hydro (207-945-6264). **Water**: Bangor Water District (207-947-4516). **Telephone**: Verizon (800-585-4466). **Cable TV**: Adelphia (800-336-9988). **Internet Service Providers**: Prexar (207-974-4300) and Mid-Maine Communications (207-992-9955).

Bangor Public Library is one of the city's most recognizable landmarks.

PHOTO BY TAMMI YOUNGBLOOD

Bangor Public Library
145 Harlow Street, Bangor

Hours:
Labor Day to Flag Day:
Monday through Thursday, 9:00 a.m. to 9:00 p.m.
Friday and Saturday, 9:00 a.m. to 5:00 p.m.
Summer:
Monday through Thursday, 9:00 a.m. to 7:00 p.m.
Friday, 9:00 a.m. to 5:00 p.m.

Bangor Public Library dates back to seven volumes kept in a foot-locker back in 1830. By 1911, the library had 70,000 volumes, making it the largest public library in the state, but a disastrous fire in April of that year swept it all away. City residents were determined to rebuild, and in 1912, the cornerstone for the new library was laid. The building was opened for public use in 1913 and continues to be an active part of the Bangor community, serving as a community center offering meeting space, providing programs for adults and children, and hosting monthly exhibits of art and artifacts. An average of 1,448 books and other items are checked out of the library every day. For more information, visit www.bpl.lib.me.us.

♠ PLACES OF WORSHIP

There are close to forty churches in Bangor, including several synagogues, as well as Bangor Theological Seminary with its charming chapel.

♠ EVENTS AND FESTIVALS

The Bangor State Fair (207-947-5555; www.bangorstatefair.com) runs from the last week of July through the first week of August and is one of the oldest agricultural fairs in the country. The Penobscot Theatre Company's annual Maine Shakespeare Festival, held at the Bangor Opera House, takes place evenings from mid-July to mid-August (207-942-3333; www.MaineShakespeare.com). The National Folk Festival (www.nationalfolkfestival.com) features lots of great— and free—music.

♠ RESTAURANTS

Almost every ethnic cuisine is represented in Bangor, from Italian to Thai, Chinese to Mexican. Along with Momma Baldacci's Italian Restaurant (207-945-5813), owned by the Maine governor John Baldacci's family, there's the landmark Miller's, home of a famous buffet (207-942-6361).

♠ LODGING

Bangor's lodging establishments are primarily chain and smaller hotels and motels, such as Country Inn at the Mall (207-541-0200), Fairfield Inn by Marriott (207-990-0001), and Riverside Inn (207-973-4100).

♠ WHAT THE LOCALS SAY

"I live in a private apartment at Boyd Place, a congregate housing area downtown," says a retired schoolteacher from La Jolla, California. "I moved here in June of 2001, to be closer to my children, several of whom live in the area."

"We'd vacationed here as a family in the summers, when my children were young, so I knew the state somewhat. My concerns before moving were mostly about the cold, changeable weather. I came from the most temperate climate in the country! I'd lived in paradise, just four blocks from the ocean."

After moving to Bangor, this retiree discovered a few surprises. "People are warm and friendly here," she says. "And Maine is beautiful." Although she cannot quite warm up to Maine's chilly temperatures, she admits to loving "the ever-changing clouds" that come with the New England climate. On the downside, she's found that Bangor's sidewalks are not always in the best condition for those who enjoy walking.

Despite these concerns, this former Californian enjoys her new city and its activities and participates in yoga classes at the Hammond Street Senior Center. "The Senior Center with its state-of-the-art fitness center is wonderful," she says. "The Bangor Public Library is very impressive, and I love having the university and so many art galleries nearby."

"If weather is not a consideration, Bangor is a fine place. It's a bit of a city, without the rush and bustle of a big metropolis. From Bangor one can also go many places in all directions and find beautiful nature as well as cultural events. Personally, I think Bangor is on the upswing."

▲▲▲

Dover-Foxcroft   *Piscataquis County*

At a Glance

Land Area: 68.23 square miles
Persons per Square Mile: 61
Population: 4,211
Median Age: 41.4 years
Neighboring Communities: Guilford, Milo, Dexter, Sebec

The shire town of Piscataquis County, Dover-Foxcroft is the gateway to Maine's North Woods, a tidy little town with shady streets and stately old homes nestled in the hills thirty-eight miles from Bangor. The Piscataquis River weaves through the downtown, and Routes 15, 153, and 7 all converge here. There are a Civil War memorial, a white-steepled Congregational Church, and a historic downtown with little mom-and-pop businesses. Sidewalked streets such as North, South, and West Main are lined with all the essentials of small-town living: the Town Hall, the hardware store, the Town Office, and a cozy little café. In other words, Dover-Foxcroft is a classic-looking New England town.

The town's hyphenated name came about when the communities of Dover and Foxcroft merged in 1915, an event recognized by a symbolic marriage ceremony that took place the night before. Today, the town is a primarily residential and commercial community with its own police department, fire department, several churches, and service organizations. It's an outdoorsy place with activities for every season. There are kayaking and canoeing on the river and lake, fishing, hunting, and hiking, along with all kinds of winter sports, including ice fishing, snowmobile riding, and Nordic and alpine skiing.

Unlike some small Maine towns, Dover-Foxcroft has its own well-respected community hospital. Mayo Regional Hospital has forty-six acute-care beds along with twenty physicians and 260 staff members dedicated to providing medical/surgical care, intensive care, and obstetrics in an inpatient setting as well as a wide array of outpatient services. "Dover," as some locals call it, takes great pride in its new YMCA as well as its private school, Foxcroft Academy, which serves the youth of the town.

As the retiree profiled later in this chapter mentions, there is not much in the way of culture right in Dover-Foxcroft. For most people here, the pristine lake, beautiful river, and gently rolling hills more than make up for the lack of restaurants and museums. Besides, Bangor with its many cultural offerings is only a forty-five-minute drive away. For some, that distance is a small price to pay for the beauty of this part of Maine.

⚑ WEATHER
Average Temperature (degrees Fahrenheit): January, 12.1; April, 38.1; July, 66; October, 43.3. **Average Annual Rainfall:** 41.05 inches. **Average Annual Snowfall:** 78.2 inches

⚑ TAXES
Property Tax Rate: $21.34 per $1,000 valuation. **Ratio to Current Market Value:** 91%.

Homes and businesses line East Main Street in Dover-Foxcroft.

PHOTO COURTESY OF THE
SOUTHERN PISCATAQUIS COUNTY
CHAMBER OF COMMERCE

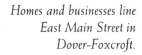

⚑ REAL ESTATE

Provided by Neil Mallett of Mallett Real Estate (207-564-8073)
Older Housing Stock: $130,000 to $150,000, depending on location. **New Custom Construction**: $150,000 to $200,000 and up, depending on size and location. **Waterfront Locations**: $150,000 to $225,000. **Riverfront Lots**: Not available. **Rental Apartments**: $400 to $500/month.

⚑ RETIREMENT COMMUNITIES

Thayer Parkway Retirement Homes has fifty-six independent-living apartments (207-564-0120). Maine West (207-564-8129) offers assisted living.

⚑ PUBLIC SAFETY

Crimes per 1,000 Population, 2000: 32.76. **Non-emergency Police**: 207-564-8021. **Non-emergency Fire**: 207-564-3318. **Emergency**: 911.

> *Our tree-shaded streets, stately turn-of-the-century homes, modern hospital, and YMCA, combined with the natural beauty of Sebec Lake and the Piscataquis River, all make Dover-Foxcroft a wonderful place to retire.*
>
> —Neil Mallett,
> Mallett Real Estate

Dennis A. Dyer, Dover-Foxcroft's chief of police, describes his town as "a safe, close-knit community. It's the kind of place where we know just about everybody by their first names. We have a twenty-four-hour department, and we work well with the people up here. I think anyone moving to Dover-Foxcroft would be proud to part of such a great community."

⚑ HEALTH CARE

Closest Hospitals: Mayo Regional Hospital is a nonprofit, forty-six-bed, acute-care facility (207-564-8401; www.mayohospital.com) in

Dover-Foxcroft. **Long-Term Care Facilities**: Hibbard's Nursing Home (207-564-8129), Fairview Manor (207-564-2014), Hilltop Manor (207-564-3049).

♦ CONTINUING EDUCATION

Senior College: Closest is in Bangor, Penobscot Valley Senior College (207-581-1947).**Colleges and Universities**: Penquis Higher Education Center (800-590-2842) offers programs through Eastern Maine Technical College and the University of Maine System. **Adult Education Programs**: SAD #68 (207-564-6525).

♦ LIBRARY

Thompson Free Library (207-564-3350).

♦ HISTORICAL SOCIETY

Dover-Foxcroft Historical Society (207-564-7137).

♦ SPECIFICALLY FOR SENIORS

Piscataquis Regional YMCA (207-564-7111) offers special programming for seniors.

♦ VOLUNTEERING

Sebec Lake Association (www.sebeclakeassoc.com) welcomes help, as do Mayo Regional Hospital (207-564-8401; www.mayohospital.com) and Friends of Thompson Public Library (207-564-3350).

♦ RECREATION

Golf: The Foxcroft Golf Club's tree-lined fairways create a challenge for all levels of players (207-564-8887). **Tennis Courts**: At Foxcroft Academy. **Parks**: Kiwanis Park has a mix of open space and wooded areas, with a brook flowing through the park. During winter months,

The Thompson Free Library was built in memory of Lucia Eddy Thompson, wife of a Union Army surgeon, in 1897.

PHOTO COURTESY OF THE SOUTHERN PISCATAQUIS COUNTY CHAMBER OF COMMERCE

the park can be reached by cross-country skiers along an abandoned railroad bed. Low's Covered Bridge is another pretty spot in Dover-Foxcroft. **Running/Walking/Biking**: Peaks-Kenny State Park on Sebec Lake. **Fitness Classes**: Piscataquis Regional YMCA (207-564-7111). **Horses/Riding**: Fox Run Riding School (207-564-3451). **Hunting/ Fishing**: Call the Town Office for licenses at 207-564-3318; www .dover-foxcroft.org). **Skiing**: Downhill and cross-country ski trails are found at Saddleback Ski Resort in Rangeley (207-695-1000).

⚑ ENTERTAINMENT

Cinemas: Northern Lights Cinema is on Route 16. **Museums**: The Blacksmith Museum dates from 1863 and is a restored shop with much original equipment. **Theaters**: The Center Theatre will soon be renovated and reopened as a performing arts center.

♠ NATURE

Peaks-Kenny State Park is on lovely Sebec Lake and has a sand beach, hiking trails, and great fishing. In-town Kiwanis Park has wooded nature areas.

♠ SHOPPING

Supermarkets are located right in Dover-Foxcroft. The nearest mall is in Bangor. A number of small specialty stores are located downtown, including Bragdon's Flower Shop (207-564-2701), Calico Corner Gift Shop (207-564-8866), and Cross Antiques (207-564-7781).

♠ WHO LIVES HERE

Population: 4,211. **Median Age:** 41.4. **Percentage Age 62 and Older:** 19.9%. **Percentage with Bachelor's Degree:** 10.7%. **Percentage with Graduate or Professional Degree:** 6.4%. **Median Household Income:** $30,164. **Mean Retirement Income:** $11,039. **Per Capita Income:** $14,544.

♠ ESSENTIAL PHONE NUMBERS AND WEB SITES

Chamber of Commerce: Southern Piscataquis County Chamber of Commerce (207-564-7533; www.spccc.org). **Town Office:** 207-564-3318; www.dover-foxcroft.org. **Voter and Vehicle Registration:** Town Clerk's Department (207-564-3318). **Drivers' Licenses:** Closest Motor Vehicle Office is in Bangor (207-942-1319).

♠ LOCAL NEWS

Newspapers: *Piscataquis Observer* (207-564-8355). **Community Internet Sites:** *The Daily ME* (www.thedailyme.com) is an online only, nonprofit newspaper. Other sites include www.dover-foxcroft.org and www.dover-foxcroft.com.

⚊ TRANSPORTATION

Bus: In Bangor. **Closest Airport**: Charles A. Chase, Jr. Memorial Field. **Traffic**: Usually light; moderate in season.

⚊ DISTANCE TO OTHER CITIES

Portland, Me. 128.9 miles

Bangor, Me. 36.7 miles

Boston, Mass. 240.3 miles

New York, N.Y. 445.1 miles

Montreal, Quebec 272.2 miles

Quebec City, Quebec 193.2 miles

Thompson Free Library

186 East Main Street, Dover-Foxcroft

Hours:

Tuesday and Thursday, 10:00 a.m. to 8:00 p.m.

Wednesday and Friday, 10:00 a.m. to 5:00 p.m.

Saturday, 10:00 a.m. to 2:00 p.m.

In 1897, Dr. Elbridge A. Thompson, a former surgeon for the Union Army, purchased land and began construction of Thompson Free Library in memory of his wife, Lucia Eddy Thompson. On September 9, 1898, he presented the town of Dover with the key and deed to the library, as well as a trust fund for the purchase of books and other materials. The library has continued to grow over the past 100 years, with a major addition in 1972. It now boasts 19,496 adult books, 981 videos, 607 books on tape, and more than 6,000 children's and young-adult books. The library provides such services as photocopying, faxing, interlibrary loan, and Internet access. For more information, see www.dover-foxcroft.org/lib.

⚑ JOBS

Dover-Foxcroft is one of fourteen communities and three unorganized territories in the Dover-Foxcroft Labor Market. Annual figures for the area in 2001 were: **Civilian Labor Force:** 7,100; **Employed:** 6,630; **Unemployed:** 470; **Unemployment Rate:** 6.7%.

⚑ UTILITIES

Electricity: Central Maine Power (800-750-4000). **Water:** Dover-Foxcroft Water District. **Telephone:** Verizon (800-585-4466). **Cable TV:** Adelphia (800-336-9988). **Internet Service Providers:** Adelphia (800-336-9988).

⚑ PLACES OF WORSHIP

Dover-Foxcroft has ten churches of various denominations. Contact the Jewish Federation for the closest synagogues (207-773-7254).

Downtown Dover-Foxcroft on an early spring day. PHOTO COURTESY OF THE SOUTHERN PISCATAQUIS COUNTY CHAMBER OF COMMERCE

▲ EVENTS AND FESTIVALS

Numerous festivals take place throughout the year, including the town's annual Homecoming Celebration, held the first Saturday in August of each year. The Piscataquis Heritage Festival (207-564-7533; www.heartofmaine.com) takes place on Columbus Day weekend.

▲ RESTAURANTS

Several fast food restaurants and ice cream parlors are in town, as are these restaurants: Moon Hing, the Bears Den, and North Meets South.

▲ LODGING

Places to stay in Dover-Foxcroft include Nelson's Guest Rooms (207-564-8568) and Peaks-Kenny Motor Lodge (207-564-0700).

▲ WHAT THE LOCALS SAY

"We chose Dover-Foxcroft for its centralized location and proximity to Bangor and the Maine Center for the Arts. The town's varied geography, mountains, rolling hills, and accessibility to outdoor activities all appealed to us. It also has a 'safe' small-town feel, which we enjoy."

A former advertising executive, this woman and her husband moved to Dover-Foxcroft from Michigan and bought a year-round home. "Although we had spent time in midcoast Maine, we weren't familiar with this area, and we didn't have any family here," she says.

"Before moving, I was concerned that the town would be too remote, but I have found that its central location is very convenient. I also wondered whether there were enough businesses such as restaurants here, and this has proven to be a real concern." She thinks that the area is somewhat economically depressed and notes a lack of quality shopping and restaurants. "On the positive side, we have one of the top regional hospitals in the state and an outstanding high school, Foxcroft Academy.

"We ought to have been more familiar with the retail and food services available," she admits, and she advises anyone considering retirement in Maine to "take the time to explore the entire state, including downtown areas and medical offerings—as well as the tax base. Ask yourself if you can afford to live in this state, which we don't find very tax-friendly. As for Dover-Foxcroft, some might find it too remote; we don't, but I would examine all aspects of the town and what it has to offer before making any decision."

▲▲▲

Down East

The counties of Hancock and Washington together comprise what is known as the Down East coast. Hancock, named for John Hancock, the first governor of Massachusetts, is probably best known for the resort town of Bar Harbor (year-round population about 4,600) and its popular neighbor, Acadia National Park. A series of rugged peninsulas that jut far into the Atlantic, this area of hidden coves, tranquil harbors, and traditional villages bustles during the summer and early fall but quiets down once the tourists depart. Meanwhile, Washington County, named for the father of our country and nicknamed the "Sunrise County" due to its eastern location, is tranquil pretty much all year. A trip through this part of Maine reveals acres and acres of windswept blueberry barrens, cornerstone of Maine's thriving lowbush blueberry industry. The coastline offers rocky and sandy beaches as well as Cobscook and Passamaquoddy Bays, with their dramatic 14-foot tides. Although there are miles and miles of oceanfront here, communities such as Calais, Eastport, Lubec, and Machias remain sparsely populated, even for Maine.

The Hancock County towns of Castine, Blue Hill, and Ellsworth are lovely spots in which to retire, and are profiled on the following pages. Castine and Blue Hill share a peninsula and the kind of small-town coastal life for which Maine is known. Ellsworth, Hancock's largest city as well as the county seat, has an active downtown in addition to convenient outlet stores. With its more affordable homes located both in the center and outside of town, Ellsworth offers the beauty of the Down East coast on a budget many seniors can afford.

Blue Hill

Hancock County

At a Glance

Land Area: 62.52 square miles
Persons per Square Mile: 38
Population: 2,390
Median Age: 44 years
Neighboring Communities: Surry, Sedgwick, Brooklin

This sweet village of white wooden buildings, many of them on the National Register of Historic Places, takes its name from the high, rounded hill overlooking Blue Hill Bay. It's a quiet town with a disproportionate number of artists and musicians as well as those who appreciate the fruits of their labors. Organizations such as the Bagaduce Music Library, an association offering musical scores to the public worldwide, thrive in Blue Hill, as does Kneisel Hall, a summer music school that holds an annual chamber music festival that brings musicians young and old to the tiny town. As you might expect in this tuneful place, there's a spirited pops concert every Fourth of July.

Blue Hill, encompassing East Blue Hill and Blue Hill Falls, was established in 1789, with shipbuilding as its first prosperous industry. Between 1792 and 1882, 133 vessels—most of them schooners—were built here, and carried lumber, masts, shingles, and seafood to Atlantic coastal cities. Even the town's first minister, Parson Jonathan Fisher, was part of the shipping business, sending cranberries to Boston aboard Blue Hill vessels. Known locally as "the Thomas Jefferson of Maine," Jonathan Fisher was a Renaissance man whose Tenney Hill home is now a museum.

Although the village's first "rusticator" arrived about 1882, to this day most tourists bypass the Blue Hill Peninsula in favor of Mount Desert Island, farther down east. They miss out on a quaint little downtown full of interesting shops and great eateries such as elegant Jean-Paul's Bistro. There are half a dozen galleries and almost as many artisan shops, plus antique stores such as Blue Hill Antiques on Water Street.

For retirees, this part of the peninsula has much to offer. Just south of town is the ninety-two-acre Parker Ridge Retirement Community, offering private apartments, assisted-living suites, and cottage residences with stunning views of Blue Hill Bay. Along with many amenities, residents enjoy the convenience of van service into town. In terms of health care, Blue Hill Memorial Hospital, renovated in 2000 to include a new ambulatory surgery department, emergency department, lobby, and pharmacy, is the centerpiece of an award-winning primary health care system and offers the benefits of affiliation with the region's tertiary-care facility, Eastern Maine Medical Center. Add to these advantages the emphasis on the arts and the area's natural beauty, and the result is hard to resist. As Parker Ridge resident Liz Knowlton observes, "I don't think there's anyone who visits Blue Hill who doesn't want to return."

♣ WEATHER
Average Temperature (degrees Fahrenheit): January, 20.4; April, 42.7; July, 68; October, 48. **Average Annual Rainfall:** 45.77 inches. **Average Annual Snowfall:** 65 inches.

♣ TAXES
Property Tax Rate: $10.50 per $1,000 valuation. **Ratio to Current Market Value:** 100%.

♣ REAL ESTATE
Provided by Bonnie Paulas, Saltmeadow Properties Real Estate (207-374-5124)
Older Housing Stock: $125,000 to $395,000, depending on location. **New Custom Construction:** $200,000 and up, depending on

size and location. **Waterfront Locations**: $300,000. **Riverfront Lots**: $125,000. **Rental Apartments**: $600/month.

⚑ RETIREMENT COMMUNITIES

Parker Ridge (207-374-5789; www.parkerridge.com) has independent-living apartments, cottages, and assisted-living units.

⚑ PUBLIC SAFETY

Crimes per 1,000 Population for Hancock County, 2000: 23.78. **Non-emergency Police**: 207-667-7575. **Non-emergency Fire**: 207-374-2261. **Emergency**: 911.

Richard Bishop, chief deputy at the Hancock County Sheriff's Office, says, "Blue Hill is certainly not a high-crime area. It gets a lot of coverage because it's what we call a 'through' town, meaning people drive through it on their way to Deer Isle. There are the

The Gazebo at Parker Ridge, a 92-acre retirement community with views of Blue Hill Bay. PHOTO BY VERENA STOLL

The main entrance of Blue Hill Memorial Hospital.

PHOTO BY BARBARA BRADY

occasional vandalism and criminal mischief, same as any small town, but on the whole, it is low-key and pretty safe."

♣ HEALTH CARE

Closest Hospitals: Blue Hill Memorial Hospital (207-374-2836; www.bhmh.org) was New England's first federally designated "Critical Access Hospital." It specializes in providing diagnostic, rehabilitative, and acute-care services. **Home Health Care**: Hancock County Home-Care (207-374-5510) offers a comprehensive continuum of individualized care to ease a patient's transition from hospital to home or to provide the assistance a patient needs to remain at home.

♣ CONTINUING EDUCATION

Senior College: Acadia Senior College operates in partnership with University College at Ellsworth (207-667-3897; www.maine.edu /ellsworth/ASC). **Adult Education Programs**: School Department (207-374-9927).

♣ LIBRARY

Blue Hill Public Library (207-374-5515).

♠ HISTORICAL SOCIETY
207-374-5596 or 207-326-8250.

♠ SPECIFICALLY FOR SENIORS
Blue Hill Memorial Hospital sponsors programs through its Health
Education Department. Call 207-374-2836, ext. 2131, for information.

♠ VOLUNTEERING
The Blue Hill Public Library (207-374-5515) and Blue Hill Memorial
Hospital (207-374-2836) welcome volunteers.

♠ RECREATION
Golf: Blue Hill Country Club is a private, nine-hole course (207-374-
2271). **Tennis Courts**: At George Stevens Academy. **Parks**: Blue Hill

---

Blue Hill Public Library
P.O. Box 824
5 Parker Point Road, Blue Hill

Hours:
Tuesday through Friday, 10:00 a.m. to 6:00 p.m.
Thursday, 10:00 a.m. to 8:00 p.m., Saturday, 10:00 a.m. to 2:00 p.m.

Blue Hill Public Library serves the people of the Blue Hill Peninsula
as a dynamic cultural center, preserving the past while exploring
the future. Newer multimedia technologies are integrated with traditional collections of books, maps, periodicals, and newspapers.
The library sponsors lectures and discussion groups, hosts community meetings, exhibits displays of local history and contemporary art, and hosts a foreign film festival. Interlibrary loan, Internet
access, photocopying, and reference help are among the services
provided. For more information, see www.bluehill.lib.me.us.

Town Park. **Running/Walking/Biking**: Thanks to area residents, a new half-mile trail winds from Parker Point Road to South Street. In addition, several trails ascend Blue Hill (the small mountain that rises above the village). **Fitness Classes**: Blue Hill Memorial Hospital (207-374-2836; www.bhmh.org) offers fitness programs at locations around the peninsula. **Hunting/Fishing**: Call the Town Office for licenses at 207-374-2281. **Skiing**: Residents cross-country ski on the golf course. The closest downhill ski area is the Camden Snow Bowl (207-236-3438).

♣ ENTERTAINMENT

Cinemas: Closest is in Ellsworth. **Museums**: Jonathan Fisher Memorial (207-374-2459), Jonathan Holt House. **Music**: Bagaduce Chorale, Blue Hill Concert Association, Kneisel Hall (207-374-2811; www.kneisel.org), Surry Opera (207-667-2629).

♣ NATURE

Holbrook Island Sanctuary on Cape Rosier in Brooksville is a great place for birdwatching.

♣ SHOPPING

Small grocery stores are found in Blue Hill; larger supermarkets are located in Bucksport and Ellsworth. The nearest mall is in Bangor. Several great little stores, such as the Blue Hill Wine Shop (207-374-2161) and Fairwinds Florist (207-374-5621), line Main Street; galleries and artisans' shops that make their home here include Rowantrees Pottery (207-374-5535) and Peninsula Weavers (207-374-2760).

♣ WHO LIVES HERE

Population: 2,390. **Median Age**: 44.7. **Percentage Age 62 and Older**: 21.4%. **Percentage with Bachelor's Degree**: 20.6%.

Percentage with Graduate or Professional Degree: 13.7%. **Median Household Income**: $31,484. **Mean Retirement Income**: $14,490. **Per Capita Income**: $19,189.

⚑ ESSENTIAL PHONE NUMBERS AND WEB SITES
Chamber of Commerce: Blue Hill Peninsula Chamber of Commerce (207-374-3242; www.bluehillmaine.com). **Town Office**: 207-374-2281. **Voter and Vehicle Registration**: Town Clerk's Department (207-374-2281). **Drivers' Licenses**: Motor Vehicle Office in Ellsworth (207-667-9363).

⚑ LOCAL NEWS
Newspapers: *The Weekly Packet* (207-374-2341). **Community Internet Sites**: www.bluehillmaine.com.

⚑ TRANSPORTATION
Bus: Closest is in Belfast. **Closest Airport**: Trenton has a small airport; Bangor International is the closest large airport. **Traffic**: The village center can be crowded in the summer months.

⚑ DISTANCE TO OTHER CITIES
Portland, Me. 133.4 miles
Bangor, Me. 39.5 miles
Boston, Mass. 244.8 miles
New York, N.Y. 449.6 miles
Montreal, Quebec 318 miles
Quebec City, Quebec 258.4 miles

⚑ JOBS
Blue Hill is one of eleven communities in the Stonington Labor Market. Annual figures for the area in 2001 were: **Civilian Labor**

Force: 5,860; Employed: 5,680; Unemployed: 180; Unemployment Rate: 3.1%.

♠ UTILITIES
Electricity: Central Maine Power (800-750-4000). Water: Mostly private wells. Telephone: Verizon (800-585-4466). Cable TV: Adelphia (800-336-9988). Internet Service Providers: HyperMedia (207-359-6573).

♠ PLACES OF WORSHIP
The churches of Blue Hill are: East Blue Hill Village Church (207-326-8331), First Congregational Church (207-374-2891), South Blue Hill Baptist Church (207-359-9858), St. Francis by the Sea Episcopal (207-374-5200), First Baptist Church of Blue Hill (207-667-3024), and Blue Hill Pentecostal Assembly (207-469-0751).

♠ EVENTS AND FESTIVALS
A popular Blue Hill event is the Kneisel Hall Chamber Music Festival (207-374-2811; www.kneisel.org). The Blue Hill Fair, held in September, features harness racing, a midway, livestock competitions, and old-time treats to eat.

♠ RESTAURANTS
Dine out in Blue Hill at Jean-Paul's Bistro on Main Street (207-374-5852), at chic Jean-Paul's at the Firepond (207-374-5851), or at Arbor Vine (207-374-2119).

♠ LODGING
Here are some places to stay in Blue Hill: The Blue Hill Inn (207-374-2844), Captain Isaac Merrill Inn (207-374-2555), and Heritage Motor Inn (207-374-5646).

⚡ WHAT THE LOCALS SAY

Liz Knowlton and her husband moved to Blue Hill in 1995 from Goshen, New York. "We had a long connection with Maine," says Liz. "My husband's father was from Deer Isle, and we visited in the summer for years and years. When we heard about Parker Ridge Retirement Community in Blue Hill, we were very enthusiastic."

The Knowltons had no concerns about moving to Maine. "Winters in Goshen were only modestly milder, so we weren't worried about that. Also, we'd attended many informational meetings at Parker Ridge, and we knew what to expect. We even watched the building going on. We were very enthusiastic about making the move."

Liz has become involved both at Parker Ridge, where she is president of the Board of Directors, and in the village, especially at her church. "Some residents of Parker Ridge are very active in town affairs, at the historical society, and at the library, for instance." She notes that if a retiree wants to become involved, there are plenty of opportunities.

Liz stresses that she and her husband were familiar with the concept of a retirement community.

> *Blue Hill is your typical New England down-home town. It's small enough so you can form a feeling of belonging to the community, and yet the arts are very important here.*
>
> —Bonnie Paulas,
> Saltmeadow Properties Real Estate

"My parents lived in one in Florida, so we were acquainted with this kind of life. I personally feel strongly that people wait too long before moving into a retirement community. They wait until they are quite elderly and thereby miss the whole point. There is so much to be said for being free of the responsibilities of snow shoveling, fixing the roof, and mowing the lawn. It's delightful to leave those chores behind. And yet our kids and grandkids visit regularly, and we are very active. It's the best of both worlds."

Castine
Hancock County

At a Glance

Land Area: 7.68 square miles
Persons per Square Mile: 174
Population: 1,343
Median Age: 23.8 years
Neighboring Communities: Orland, Penobscot, Brooksville

The small coastal village of Castine is perched on the tip of a narrow spit of land on the Blue Hill Peninsula, part of Maine's East Penobscot Bay region. Located at the confluence of two rivers, the town consists of two distinct geographic areas referred to as the village and "off neck," a narrow strip of land that separates the Bagaduce River on one side from the Penobscot River on the other.

Castine is steeped in history. First settled in 1604, the town is one of the oldest in the state of Maine and once served as a trading post for the Pilgrims. The village has been owned by more countries than perhaps any place in the United States. Baron de Saint Castine, a French nobleman who married a Penobscot Indian princess, lent the town his name, but rights to the area would be swapped back and forth, as the years went on, between the French, British, Americans, and even the Dutch. Today, Castine is on the National Register of Historic Places, and more than 100 historic markers can be found among the perfectly preserved examples of eighteenth-century architecture. Major landmarks include Fort George, built by the British in 1779 and partially restored as a state memorial; and Fort Madison, an earthwork structure built by the Americans in 1811, occupied by the British during the War of 1812, and reconstructed during the American Civil War.

As a glance at a map shows, this picturesque village is more accessible by sea than by land. But for all its remoteness, Castine has

223

a surprisingly diverse population, thanks in large part to the roughly 700 college students who attend Maine Maritime Academy, the town's biggest employer and an international leader in maritime studies.

With the long days of summer comes an influx of summer residents, yachting visitors, and day-trippers, doubling the town's population. Despite its appeal as a tourist destination, the town has an authentic New England feel to it, complete with white-steepled churches, elm-shaded streets, village green, and working harbor. It's a social town, too, with friendly golf, tennis, yacht, and garden clubs. During the colder months, the socializing continues indoors at Maine Maritime's fitness facilities, where the community is generously given access through paid memberships.

Castine enjoys public access to the waterfront, too, including Dyce's Head Lighthouse and a welcoming town dock outfitted with picnic tables and restrooms. "Not only do we have beautiful scenery,"

Maine Maritime Academy's training ship State of Maine *is at her berth on the* Castine waterfront. PHOTO BY JANICE ZENTER, COURTESY OF MAINE MARITIME ACADEMY

says local realtor Karen Koos, "but we're fortunate to have easy access to the bay." She notes that the town is a destination for yacht clubs from all over. "Who wouldn't want to come here? It's a wonderful place."

♣ WEATHER
Average Temperature (degrees Fahrenheit): January, 20.4; April, 42.7; July, 68; October, 48. **Average Annual Rainfall**: 45.77 inches. **Average Annual Snowfall**: 65 inches.

♣ TAXES
Property Tax Rate: $8.18 per $1,000 valuation. **Ratio to Current Market Value**: 100%.

♣ REAL ESTATE
Provided by Karen Koos, Saltmeadow Properties Real Estate (207-326-9116)
Older Housing Stock: $269,000 to $1,450,000, depending on location. **New Custom Construction**: $125 per square foot and up, depending on size and location. **Waterfront Locations**: $895,000. **Rental Apartments**: $800/month.

♣ RETIREMENT LIVING
Parker Ridge Retirement Community (207-374-5789; www .parkerridge.com) in nearby Blue Hill has independent-living apartments, cottages, and assisted-living units.

♣ PUBLIC SAFETY
Crimes per 1,000 Population for Hancock County, 2000: 23.78. **Non-emergency Police**: 207-667-7576. **Non-emergency Fire**: 207-326-8767. **Emergency**: 911.

Richard Bishop, chief deputy at the Hancock County Sheriff's Office, says, "Castine is a laid-back, unique kind of place. We work hand in hand with Maine Maritime on education and programs that help to keep the town as safe as possible."

▲ HEALTH CARE
Closest Hospitals: Blue Hill Memorial Hospital (207-374-2836; www.bhmh.org). Bagaduce Area Health Resources (207-326-8005) provides transportation for medical appointments, prescription pickup, and a loaner program for durable medical equipment. There is no fee for any of the organization's services. Castine Community Health Services (207-326-4348) offers care as well as a twenty-four-hour emergency clinic and assisted-living services through Hancock County Home Care.

▲ CONTINUING EDUCATION
Senior College: Acadia Senior College operates in partnership with University College at Ellsworth (207-667-3897: www.maine.edu/ellsworth/ASC). **Colleges and Universities:** Maine Maritime Academy (207-326-4311; www.mainemaritime.edu). **Adult Education Programs:** None in Castine; residents go to Bucksport or Blue Hill.

▲ LIBRARY
Witherle Memorial Library (207-326-4375).

▲ HISTORICAL SOCIETY
Castine Historical Society (207-326-4118).

▲ SPECIFICALLY FOR SENIORS
The Recreation Committee sponsors courses—some of which are held in the Town Hall—and is in the process of starting a social club. The Castine Women's Club sponsors a monthly luncheon for seniors as well. Contact the Town Office at 207-326-4502 for more information.

↟ VOLUNTEERING

The Conservation Trust (207-326-9711), Friends of Witherle Memorial Library (207-326-4375), and Castine Garden Club (207-326-8020) all welcome volunteers.

↟ RECREATION

Golf: Castine Golf Club (207-326-8844). **Tennis Courts**: At Maine Maritime Academy (207-326-4311). **Parks**: Fort George, built by the British in 1779, is a state memorial. **Running/Walking/Biking**: Witherle Woods. **Fitness Classes**: At Maine Maritime Academy (207-326-4311). **Hunting/Fishing**: Call the Town Office for licenses at 207-326-4502. **Skiing**: Cross-country skiers blaze trails on the

---

Witherle Memorial Library
P.O. Box 202
41 School Street, Castine

Hours:
Monday, 4:00 to 8:00 p.m.
Tuesday through Friday, 11:00 a.m. to 5:00 p.m.
Saturday, 11:00 a.m. to 2:00 p.m.

In 1855, Castine became the first community in Maine to establish a public library supported by public funds. The present-day building was completed in 1913, the gift of George H. and Mary H. Witherle, ship chandlers in Castine. The library, listed on the National Register of Historical Places, has nearly 13,000 volumes and offers a full range of services, including free public Internet access, interlibrary loan, delivery of books to shut-ins, collections of audio books, music on compact disc, videos, an extensive local history collection, and photocopying. For more information, see www.witherle.lib.me.us.

---

course at the Castine Golf Club. The closest downhill ski area is the Camden Snow Bowl (207-236-3438).

♣ ENTERTAINMENT
Cinemas: None, although Maine Maritime Academy shows occasional films. **Museums**: Wilson Museum (207-326-8545).

Castine is a wonderful retirement choice. It's a diverse, friendly, and caring community with easy-to-join clubs, four churches, a full-time health center, historical society, and very active land trusts. Plus, we have the use of Maine Maritime Academy facilities such as a swimming pool, gym, and indoor tennis.

*—Karen Koos,
Saltmeadow Properties
Real Estate*

♣ NATURE
Witherle Woods "on neck" has trails. The Castine Conservation Trust owns Rene Henderson Preserve.

♣ SHOPPING
A small grocery store is located right in town, and bigger supermarkets are in Bucksport. The nearest mall is in Bangor. Castine's downtown has numerous small specialty stores, such as Dolphin Books and Prints (207-326-0888).

♣ WHO LIVES HERE
Population: 1,343. **Median Age**: 23.8. **Percentage Age 62 and Older**: 17%. **Percentage with Bachelor's Degree**: 31.3%. **Percentage with Graduate or Professional Degree**: 26.5%. **Median Household Income**: $46,250. **Mean Retirement Income**: $25,889. **Per Capita Income**: $20,078.

♣ ESSENTIAL PHONE NUMBERS AND WEB SITES
Chamber of Commerce: Blue Hill Peninsula Chamber of Commerce

(207-374-3242; www.bluehillmaine.com). **Town Office**: 207-326-4502; www.castine.me.us. **Voter and Vehicle Registration**: Town Clerk's Department (207-326-4502; www.castine.me.us). **Drivers' Licenses**: Motor Vehicle Office in Ellsworth (207-667-9363).

▲ LOCAL NEWS
Newspapers: *Castine Patriot* (207-326-9300). **Community Internet Site**: www.castine.me.us.

▲ TRANSPORTATION
Bus: Closest is in Belfast. **Closest Airport**: Trenton has a small airport; the closest large airport is in Bangor. **Traffic**: The village can be crowded in the summer months.

▲ DISTANCE TO OTHER CITIES
Portland, Me. 131.6 miles
Bangor, Me. 36.6 miles
Boston, Mass. 243 miles
New York, N.Y. 447.7 miles
Montreal, Quebec 316.2 miles
Quebec City, Quebec 256.5 miles

▲ JOBS
Castine is one of eleven communities in the Stonington Labor Market. Annual figures for the area in 2001 were: **Civilian Labor Force**: 5,860; **Employed**: 5,680; **Unemployed**: 180; **Unemployment Rate**: 3.1%.

▲ UTILITIES
Electricity: Central Maine Power (800-750-4000). **Water**: 207-326-8540. **Telephone**: Verizon (800-585-4466). **Cable TV**: Adelphia (800-336-9988). **Internet Service Providers**: HyperMedia (207-359-6573).

⚱ PLACES OF WORSHIP

There are four churches in town: Castine Unitarian Church (207-326-9083), Trinity Episcopal (207-326-0787), Our Lady of Holy Hope Catholic Church (207-469-3322), and Trinitarian Parish Church (207-326-9486).

⚱ EVENTS AND FESTIVALS

The Blue Hill Peninsula is the site of numerous festivals during the summer months. Contact the Chamber of Commerce (207-374-3242; www.bluehillmaine.com) for more information.

⚱ RESTAURANTS

Dining choices include Dennett's Wharf (207-326-9045), Reef Restaurant (207-326-4040), and Water Street Restaurant (207-326-2008).

⚱ LODGING

Two of the nicest places to stay here are The Castine Inn (207-326-4365) and the Pentagöet Inn (800-845-1701; www.pentagoet.com).

The Pentagöet Inn provides luxurious accommodations and delicious dinners.
PHOTO BY FRANCOISE GERVAIS

♠ WHAT THE LOCALS SAY

Bob and Carol Bonini came to Castine in 1998. "We started thinking about retiring when I was 52," says Bob. "In 1991 we took a trip to scout out retirement locations. We started in Wisconsin, drove through Canada, and came into Maine. We were driving down Route 1 when we saw a sign for Castine. And we decided to check it out."

The Boninis ended up buying property upon which they eventually built a house and guesthouse. "We really didn't have any concerns before we moved. There's a goodly amount of health care, so that wasn't a worry. There's plenty to do, everything from cooking classes, to big-band concerts, to golf and boating, so we knew we'd keep as busy as we wanted. This is such a diverse community that you can find all kinds of things to do."

Bob and Carol have found it easy to join town activities. Bob has volunteered at the grade school and is involved in local politics. "I'm 'from away,' but I've been accepted here," he says. "I really appreciate that."

Another plus is the diverse wildlife that the Boninis have observed on their property: "Herds of deer, a crew of turkeys, eagles, coyotes, a bobcat, a bear—not to mention all the birds at Carol's feeders," says Bob.

"Castine seems to us like a throwback to the way Maine used to be," says Bob. "It's a beautiful village, with kind, hardworking people." He admits to being one of the town's biggest boosters and says, "It's a very easy place to live."

♠♠♠

Ellsworth *Hancock County*

At a Glance

Land Area: 79.24 square miles
Persons per Square Mile: 81
Population: 6,456
Median Age: 40.5 years
Neighboring Communities: Trenton, Blue Hill, Ellsworth Falls, Hancock, Surry, Lamoine, Bar Harbor

There's a lot to like in Ellsworth. Start with a thriving downtown of old brick buildings that house offices, shops, and eateries as well as a unique and historic theater with year-long cultural events. Coastal Ellsworth is on the Union River, close to bustling Bar Harbor, and boasts Waterfront Park, home to pleasure and working craft. Tree-lined streets here border stately old homes, and yet there is plenty of rural land for quiet country drives. Facilities such as Maine Coast Memorial Hospital and University College at Ellsworth, a branch of the University of Maine, only add to the city's livability.

But that's not all. Ellsworth also has tranquil Graham Lake for fishing and boating, busy Route 3 for "big box" and outlet shopping, and Acadia Senior College to stretch the mind and imagination. There are a YMCA, several good restaurants, and Acadia National Park practically next door. Picture-perfect coastal villages such as Northeast Harbor are just a short drive away as well. Yet unlike the pretty towns of Mount Desert Island (including famous Bar Harbor), Ellsworth has a year-round economy, in part due to its status as the county's shire town.

The land on which Ellsworth sits was first settled by the Passamaquoddy and Penobscot Indians; the first English settlers arrived in 1763. The Union River, which flows through the heart of the city and into harbor-like Waterfront Park, was the economic spur of early

Ellsworth, powering sawmills and gristmills, and was first bridged in 1805. Incorporated just five years before that first bridge, Ellsworth became the seat of Hancock County in 1837.

Although Ellsworth may seem on the remote side, major highways intersect in the heart of the city and connect it to places along the coast and to the interior. Bangor is the closest "big" city, and residents point out that it's only twenty-seven miles away. "Ellsworth is one of those towns that everybody drives through on the way to Bar Harbor, but we have a lot to offer in this area," says local Joanne Cooper. "It's a great place to live."

⚑ WEATHER

Average Temperature (degrees Fahrenheit): January, 20.4; April, 42.7; July, 68; October, 48. **Average Annual Rainfall:** 45.77 inches. **Average Annual Snowfall:** 65 inches.

⚑ TAXES

Property Tax Rate: $16.88 per $1,000 valuation. **Ratio to Current Market Value:** 75% to 80%.

⚑ REAL ESTATE

Provided by Mary Purslow, Knowles Real Estate (207-667-4604)
Older Housing Stock: $80,000 to $140,000, depending on location. **New Custom Construction:** $150,000 and up, depending on size and location. **Waterfront Locations:** $150,000 and up. **Riverfront Lots:** $60,000. **Rental Apartments:** $700/month.

⚑ RETIREMENT LIVING

New housing for retirees is under construction at this writing, next to Denny's Restaurant in Ellsworth. Contact the Chamber of Commerce (207-667-5584) for more information. Meadowview Apartments (207-667-2651) offers low-income housing for seniors in Ellsworth.

Bar Harbor's Birch Bay Village (207-288-8639; www.birchbayinfo
.com) has twenty-one independent-living apartments, twenty cottage
units, and thirty-two assisted-living units.

⚓ PUBLIC SAFETY

Crimes per 1,000 Population, 2000: 57.26. **Non-emergency Police**:
207-667-2168. **Emergency Police**: 911. **Non-emergency Fire**: 207-
667-8666. **Emergency Fire**: 911.

"At 93 square miles, Ellsworth is the largest city, geographically
speaking, in the state of Maine," says Police Chief John R. DeLeo.
"As 'Crossroads to Down East Maine,' we serve as the center of Hancock County in many regards: population, retail, judicial, financial,
and governmental. We also serve as the gateway to Acadia National
Park on nearby Mount Desert Island. An abundance of rural areas
allows residents to live away from the hustle and bustle. The Police
Department takes great pride in providing a safe place for residents
to live and tourists to visit."

⚓ HEALTH CARE

Closest Hospitals: Maine Coast Memorial Hospital is a sixty-four-
bed, acute-care hospital right in Ellsworth (207-667-5311). Mount
Desert Island Hospital in Bar Harbor (207-288-5081) has fifteen
beds. **Clinics**: Coastal Health Center, 125 Oak Street, Ellsworth, ME
04605; 207-667-2422. **Long-Term Care Facilities**: Hospice of
Hancock County (207-667-2531).

⚓ CONTINUING EDUCATION

Senior College: Acadia Senior College operates in partnership with
University College at Ellsworth (207-667-3897; www.maine.edu
/ellsworth/ASC). **Colleges and Universities**: Eastern Maine Community College (207-667-5101), University College at Ellsworth

(207-667-3897). **Adult Education Programs**: Held at Hancock County Technical Center (207-667-6499).

⚑ LIBRARY
Ellsworth Public Library (207-667-6363).

⚑ HISTORICAL SOCIETY
Ellsworth Historical Society; contact Deal Salisbury (207-667-3766).

⚑ SPECIFICALLY FOR SENIORS
Down East Family YMCA (207-667-3086) offers special classes just for seniors. Hancock County Connections is starting a program to provide free services to area elderly so they can remain at home with a high quality of life; contact Joanne Cooper (207-667-7062) for more information.

The Ellsworth Public Library is an historic Federal-style building built in 1817 and located in downtown Ellsworth. PHOTO BY DARLENE BEARSE

Ellsworth Public Library
20 State Street, Ellsworth

Hours:
Monday, Tuesday, and Friday, 9:00 a.m. to 5:00 p.m.
Wednesday and Thursday, 9:00 a.m. to 8:00 p.m.
Saturday, 9:00 a.m. to 2:00 p.m.

Ellsworth Public Library is located downtown on the banks of the Union River. The Federal-style building, built in 1817, is listed on the National Register of Historic Places, and has been a public library since 1897. The library houses more than 36,000 books and audiobooks for all ages, as well as large-print books, videos, magazines, and several special collections. Services include Books-on-Call for shut-ins, interlibrary loan, and reference. For more information, see www.ellsworth.lib.me.us.

♣ VOLUNTEERING

The Friends of the Ellsworth Public Library (207-667-6363; www.ellsworth.lib.me.us) and Maine Coast Memorial Hospital (207-667-5311) are among the many Ellsworth organizations that welcome volunteers.

♣ RECREATION

Golf: The closest course, Bar Harbor Golf Course (207-667-7505) in Trenton, is just ten minutes away. **Tennis Courts**: Ellsworth Tennis Courts (207-664-0400). **Parks**: Union River Dock. **Running/Walking/Biking**: Both the Birdsacre Wildlife Sanctuary and Colonel Black Mansion have trails. **Fitness Classes**: Down East Family YMCA (207-667-3086). **Hunting/Fishing**: Call City Hall for licenses at 207-667-2563. **Skiing**: Cross-country trails are found at the Colonel Black

Mansion. Closest downhill ski area is the Camden Snow Bowl (207-236-3438).

⚑ ENTERTAINMENT

Cinemas: The Grand Theatre (207-667-9500; www.grandonline.org). **Museums:** Telephone Museum (207-667-9491); Colonel Black Mansion, a nineteenth-century home formerly inhabited by three generations of the Black family; Stanwood Homestead Museum, the 1850 home of noted ornithologist Cornelia Stanwood, adjacent to the Birdsacre Wildlife Sanctuary. **Theaters:** The Grand Theatre (207-667-9500; www.grandonline.org) presents more than fifty concerts annually, covering a breadth of musical, theatrical, and dance styles. The Grand also shows a wide selection of movies and serves as a gallery for Maine artists.

⚑ NATURE

The Birdsacre Wildlife Sanctuary in Ellsworth has forty wooded acres with eight hiking trails and three ponds.

The Grand Theatre is an art deco masterpiece as well as a gathering place for the Ellsworth community of art lovers.
PHOTO BY ANTHONY PIZZUTO

↟ SHOPPING

Supermarkets are located on Route 3, as is the L. L. Bean Outlet and several other large stores. The nearest mall is in Bangor. Downtown Ellsworth has many small specialty stores, including The Book Shelf (207-667-1120) on State Street.

↟ WHO LIVES HERE

Population: 6,456. Median Age: 40.5. Percentage Age 62 and Older: 19.3%. Percentage with Bachelor's Degree: 16.1%. Percentage with Graduate or Professional Degree: 8.7%. Median Household Income: $35,938. Mean Retirement Income: $14,501. Per Capita Income: $21,049.

↟ ESSENTIAL PHONE NUMBERS AND WEB SITES

Chamber of Commerce: 207-667-5584; www.ellsworthchamber.org. City Hall: 207-667-2563; www.ci.ellsworth.me.us. Voter and Vehicle Registration: (207-667-2563; www.ci.ellsworth.me.us/) Drivers' Licenses: Motor Vehicle Office (207-667-9363). Newcomers Organization: None, but the Chamber of Commerce is happy to help newcomers.

> *Ellsworth is uncrowded, friendly, and a great service center. We have a good hospital, varied shopping, entertainment, plus easy access to Acadia National Park and many exceptional recreational areas.*
>
> —Mary Purslow, Knowles Real Estate

↟ LOCAL NEWS

Newspapers: *The Ellsworth American* (207-667-2576; www.ellsworthamerican.com), *The Ellsworth Weekly* (207-667-5514). Community Cable Station: Channel 11. Community Internet Sites: www.ellsworthme.org, www.ci.ellsworth.me.us.

WHAT AND WHERE IS "DOWN EAST"?

Besides being the name of Maine's signature magazine, what is meant by the term *down east?* Judy Hayes, a cartographer at DeLorme Publishing, gives this definition:

"'Down east' refers to sailing downwind in an easterly direction. As a region, Down East is generally understood to extend from the eastern rim of Penobscot Bay to Lubec–Eastport."

⚓ TRANSPORTATION

Bus: Downeast Transportation offers service to Bangor (207-667-5796). **Closest Airport**: Trenton has a small airport; the closest large airport is in Bangor. **Traffic**: Route 3 is busy in season; otherwise, it is easy to get around.

⚓ DISTANCE TO OTHER CITIES

Portland, Me. 154.1 miles
Bangor, Me. 27.3 miles
Boston, Mass. 265.5 miles
New York, N.Y. 470.2 miles
Montreal, Quebec 311.7 miles
Quebec City, Quebec 252.0 miles

⚓ JOBS

Ellsworth is one of twenty-six communities and three unorganized territories in the Ellsworth–Bar Harbor Labor Market. Annual figures for the area in 2001 were: **Civilian Labor Force**: 20,980; **Employed**: 19,900; **Unemployed**: 1,090; **Unemployment Rate**: 5.2%.

⬥ UTILITIES

Electricity: Central Maine Power (800-750-4000). **Water:** 207-667-2155. **Telephone:** Verizon (800-585-4466). **Cable TV:** Adelphia (800-336-9988). **Internet Service Providers:** Adelphia (800-336-9988).

⬥ PLACES OF WORSHIP

Churches of many denominations are found in Ellsworth. The town's first church, the Congregational Church on State Street Hill, was built in 1818 by Captain Meletiah Jordan and still welcomes parishioners.

⬥ EVENTS AND FESTIVALS

Numerous festivals take place throughout the year, including Autumn Gold Weekend in September, featuring a chowder fest and antique car show.

⬥ RESTAURANTS

Eating out in Ellsworth means choosing between lots of places, such as: Jordan's Snack Bar (207-667-2174), The Mex (207-667-4494), Killarney's (207-667-9341), Sylvia's Café (207-667-7014), and the Riverside Café (207-667-7220).

⬥ LODGING

Places to stay in Ellsworth include The Eagles Lodge (207-667-3311) and The White Birches Restaurant & Motel (207-667-3621).

⬥ WHAT THE LOCALS SAY

Warren Craft retired to the Ellsworth area a decade ago. "We'd come here for forty years on vacations, mainly camping, so we knew the area well. But even though we were familiar with things, we still had some concerns. We wondered whether we would fit into the community and how we'd survive the winters."

Warren and his wife rented a house as a test run and, after a year or so, bought a home. "We realized that it was easy to fit in here. We didn't come with a belligerent attitude, wanting to change things, and I think that's the key." Warren became involved with local boards and even started a small computer business. He began teaching computer courses in the adult education program, a practice he's continued for the past eight years.

"Moving here was a little like going back in time for me," says Warren Craft. "It's the country, and I like that. It's a decent, good place to live."

He has advice for those considering a move to Hancock County: "I notice a lot of people wanting to change things up here. They need to back off. Come to Maine with an open mind and accept things the way they are for a while. Offer changes if you have to, but don't insist on them."

▲▲▲

Appendix:
Retirement Communities

Every year more retirement communities are being built or expanded. Please call or write the individual facilities for their latest information. (Data as of February 2003, provided by *Down East* magazine.)

The communities listed here all provide housekeeping services and at least one meal per day, and most can provide transportation.

Key to abbreviations in the Types of Units column:
IA = independent apartments; C = cottages;
A = Alzheimer's units; LT = long-term care beds;
AL = assisted living units.

FACILITY	Number of Residents	Distance to Hospital (miles)	Rent, Purchase or Both	Types of Units
Auburn				
Clover Health Care 440 Minot Ave., Auburn, ME 04210 207-784-3573 www.mainecare.com	270	3	R	IA, A, LT, AL
Schooner Retirement Community 200 Stetson Rd., Auburn, ME 04210 207-784-2900; 800-924-9997 www.schoonerestates.com	180	3	R	IA, AL

FACILITY	Number of Residents	Distance to Hospital (miles)	Rent, Purchase or Both	Types of Units
Bangor				
Boyd Place 21 Boyd St., Bangor ME 04401 207-941-2837 www.seniorhousing.net/ad/boydplace	85	.5	R	IA, AL
Park East Retirement Villa 146 Balsam Dr., Bangor, ME 04401 207-947-7992 www.parkeastapts.com	22	1	R	IA
Sunbury Village 922 Ohio St., Bangor ME 04401 207-262-9600 www.sunburyvillage.net	99	2	R	IA
Bar Harbor				
Birch Bay Village 10 Wyman Lane, Bar Harbor, ME 04609 207-288-8014 www.birchbayinfo.com	130	4	B	IA, C A, AL
Belfast				
Harbor Hill 2 Foot Bridge Rd., Belfast, ME 04915 207-338-5307 www.sandyriverhealth.com	82	3	R	A, LT AL
Penobscot Shores 10 Shoreland Dr., Belfast, ME 04915 207-338-2332 www.penobscotshores.com	74	.25	P	IA, C

FACILITY	Number of Residents	Distance to Hospital (miles)	Rent, Purchase or Both	Types of Units
Blue Hill				
Parker Ridge Retirement Community	71	3	B	IA, C, AL
PO Box 270, Blue Hill, ME 04614				
207-374-5789				
www.parkerridge.com				
Boothbay Harbor				
St. Andrews Village	150	1.5	B	IA, C, A, LT, AL
145 Emery Ln., Boothbay Harbor, ME 04538				
207-633-0920				
www.standrewsvillage.com				
Brewer				
Ellen M. Leach Memorial Home	96	1.5	R	IA
PO Box 359, Brewer, ME 04412				
207-989-6352				
www.leachmemorialhome.org				
Brunswick				
Thornton Oaks	254	4.8	P	IA, C, A, LT, AL
25 Thornton Way, Brunswick, ME 04011				
207-729-8033; 800-729-8033				
www.thorntonoaks.com				
Camden				
Camden Gardens	12	5	R	IA, C
110 Mechanic St., Camden, ME 04843				
207-236-0154				
Quarry Hill	207	6	B	IA, C, A, LT, AL
30 Community Dr., Camden, ME 04843				
207-236-6116				
www.quarryhill.org				

FACILITY	Number of Residents	Distance to Hospital (miles)	Rent, Purchase or Both	Types of Units
Cape Elizabeth				
Chancellor Gardens	42	4	R	AL
78 Scott Dyer Rd., Cape Elizabeth, ME 04107				
207-799-7332; 888-860-6914				
Damariscotta				
Chase Point Assisted Living	24	.1	R	A, AL
Schooner St., Damariscotta, ME 04543				
207-563-4200				
www.chasepoint.org				
Schooner Cove	55	.1	B	IA
35 Schooner St., Damariscotta, ME 04543				
207-563-5523				
www.mileshealthcare.org/schooner				
Falmouth				
OceanView at Falmouth	200	6	P	IA, C, AL
20 Blueberry Ln., Falmouth, ME 04105				
207-781-4460				
www.oceanviewrc.com				
Farmington				
Orchard Park Rehabilitation and Living Ctr.	13	5	R	IA, AL
136 North St., Farmington, ME 04938				
207-778-4416, 800-260-4416				
Gorham				
Gorham House	165	12	R	IA, C, A, LT, AL
50 New Portland Rd., Gorham, ME 04038				
207-839-5757				
www.mainecare.com				

FACILITY	Number of Residents	Distance to Hospital (miles)	Rent, Purchase or Both	Types of Units
Hallowell				
Granite Hill Estates 60 Balsam Dr., Hallowell, ME 04347 207-626-7786; 888-321-1119 www.granitehillestates.com	150	2	B	IA, C, AL
Hampden				
Avalon Village 50 Foxglove Dr., Hampden, ME 04444 207-862-5100, 800-950-0037 www.avalon-maine.com	72	4	B	IA, C AL
Houlton				
Madigan Estates 93 Military St., Houlton, ME 04730 207-532-6593 www.madiganestates.com	135	1.5	R	IA, A, LT, AL
Kennebunk				
Atria Kennebunk 1 Penny Ln., Kennebunk, ME 04043 207-985-5866 www.atriacom.com	82	7	R	A, AL
Huntington Common 1 Huntington Com. Dr., Kennebunk, ME 04043 207-985-2810; 800-585-0533 www.huntingtoncommon.com	200	4.5	R	IA, C, A, AL
The Farragut at Kennebunk 106 Farragut Way, Kennebunk, ME 04043 207-985-0300; 877-985-0300 www.thefarragut.com	70	4.5	B	IA, C

FACILITY	Number of Residents	Distance to Hospital (miles)	Rent, Purchase or Both	Types of Units
Lewiston				
Montello Heights	80	2	R	IA
550 College St., Lewiston, ME 04240				
207-786-7149				
Newcastle				
Lincoln Home	40	2	R	IA, AL
22 River Rd., Newcastle, ME 04553				
207-563-3350				
email: inquire@lincoln-home.org				
Orono				
Dirigo Pines Retirement Community	10	7	B	IA, C, A, LT, AL
PO Box 9, Orono, ME 04473				
207-866-3400				
www.dirigopines.com				
Portland				
Seventy-Five State Street	184	.1	R	IA, AL
75 State St., Portland, ME 04101				
207-772-2675				
www.seventyfivestate.com				
The Atrium at Cedars	60	2.5	P	IA
640 Ocean Ave., Portland, ME 04103				
207-775-4111				
www.atriumatcedars.com				
The Park Danforth	170	4	R	IA, AL
777 Stevens Ave., Portland, ME 04103				
207-797-7710				
www.parkdanforth.com				
The Woods at Canco Road	149	5	R	IA, C
Portland, ME 04103				
207-772-4777				

FACILITY	Number of Residents	Distance to Hospital (miles)	Rent, Purchase or Both	Types of Units
Presque Isle				
Leisure Gardens Apartments	110	60	R	IA, AL
4 Dewberry Dr., Presque Isle, ME 04769				
207-764-7322				
www.ainop.com/lgardens/				
Rockland				
Bartlett Woods	57	2.5	R	IA, C
20 Bartlett Dr., Rockland, ME 04841				AL
207-594-2745				
www.bartlettwoods.com				
Saco				
Wardwell Retirement Neighborhood	98	2.5	R	IA, AL
143 Middle St., Saco, ME 04072				
207-284-7061				
Scarborough				
Piper Shores	n/a	7	n/a	IA, C,
15 Piper Rd., Scarborough, ME 04074				LT, AL
207-883-8700; 888-333-8711				
www.pipershores.org				
Topsham				
The Highlands	285	2.5	B	IA, C,
26 Elm St., Topsham, ME 04086				A, AL
207-725-2650; 888-760-1042				
www.highlandsrc.com				
Waterville				
Park Residences	128	1	R	IA, A,
141 West River Rd., Waterville, ME 04901				AL
207-861-5685				
www.woodlandsalf.com				

FACILITY	Number of Residents	Distance to Hospital (miles)	Rent, Purchase or Both	Types of Units
Winslow				
Winslow Place	13	1.5	R	IA
36 1/2 Garand St., Winslow, ME 04901				
800-876-9212				
www.bridgesbiz.com				
Yarmouth				
Bay Square at Yarmouth	60	12	R	IA, A, AL
27 Forest Falls Dr., Yarmouth, ME 04096				
207-846-0044, 888-374-6700				
www.benchmarkquality.com				
York				
Sentry Hill	160	.5	B	IA, C, A, LT, AL
2 Victoria Ct., York, ME 03909				
207-363-5116				
www.sentryhill.com				

Index

Victoria Doudera is the author of the bestselling book, *Moving to Maine: The Essential Guide to Get You There*, published by Down East Books. She has written more than a hundred articles for national magazines including *Yankee, Parenting, Readers Digest, Maine Boats & Harbors*, and *The Old Farmer's Almanac* as well as major newspapers, and is the co-producer of an entertaining audio CD walking tour of the coastal Maine towns of Camden and Rockport.

Victoria moved to Maine from Boston, Massachusetts, in 1986 to open a country inn with her husband, attorney Edward Doudera. After twelve years in the hospitality industry, the couple sold the property and Victoria began writing full-time. Now a licensed real estate sales agent with Camden Real Estate, she lives with Ed and their three children in midcoast Maine, where she gardens, plays ice hockey, and sails the waters of Penobscot Bay.

She welcomes your comments and questions about finding property, retiring, or relocating in Maine. Contact Victoria at 207-236-6171, or vicki@camdenre.com.
Learn more about her writing career on her website, www.VictoriaDoudera.com.

PHOTO BY PATRISHA McLEAN